Self-instruction in Language Learning

NEW DIRECTIONS IN LANGUAGE TEACHING
Editors: Howard B. Altman and Peter Strevens

This important series is for language teachers and others who:
– need to be informed about the key issues facing the language teaching profession today;
– want to understand the theoretical issues underlying current debates;
– wish to relate theory to classroom practice.

In this series:

Communicative Language Teaching – An introduction
by William Littlewood

Developing Reading Skills – A practical guide to reading comprehension exercises *by Françoise Grellet*

Simulations in Language Teaching *by Ken Jones*

Video in Language Teaching *by Jack Lonergan*

Computers, Language Learning and Language Teaching
by Khurshid Ahmad, Greville Corbett, Margaret Rogers and Roland Sussex

Beyond Methodology – Second Language Teaching and the Community
by Mary Ashworth

Course Design – Developing programs and materials for language learning
by Fraida Dubin and Elite Olshtain

English for Specific Purposes – A learning-centred approach
by Tom Hutchinson and Alan Waters

Principles of Course Design for Language Teaching *by Janice Yalden*

Strategic Interaction – Learning languages through scenarios
by Robert J. Di Pietro

Self-instruction in Language Learning *by Leslie Dickinson*

Self-instruction in Language Learning

Leslie Dickinson

Cambridge University Press
Cambridge
London New York New Rochelle
Melbourne Sydney

Published by the Press Syndicate of the University of Cambridge
The Pitt Building, Trumpington Street, Cambridge CB2 1RP
32 East 57th Street, New York, NY 10022, USA
10 Stamford Road, Oakleigh, Melbourne 3166, Australia

First published 1987

Printed in Great Britain at The Bath Press, Avon

British Library cataloguing in publication data

Dickinson, Leslie
Self-instruction in language learning.
(New directions in language teaching)
1. Language and languages – Study and
teaching 2. Independent study
I. Title II. Series
407 P51

Library of Congress cataloguing in publication data

Dickinson, Leslie
Self-instruction in language learning.
(New directions in language teaching)
Bibliography: p.
Includes index.
1. Language and languages – Programmed instruction.
I. Title. II. Series.
P53.65.D5 1987 418′.007 86–26331

ISBN 0 521 26600 9 hard covers
ISBN 0 521 31967 6 paperback

BS

Contents

Foreword

It comes as no surprise to those involved with the process of learning a second or foreign language to hear that 'the age of the learner' is upon us. Language journals and papers presented at language conferences throughout much of the world have trumpeted this message for at least a decade, though there is always a considerable lag between theory and practice, between pronouncement and implementation.

In much of the flurry of activity on the topic of 'learner-centred language teaching' over the past decade, the emphasis has remained firmly placed on the traditionally organised classroom, in which a trained language teacher attempts to instruct learners, and to meet their differing needs to the extent possible. What Leslie Dickinson has contributed in this volume is perhaps the first significant discussion of how language learners can instruct themselves. Language *learning* does not necessarily presuppose that the learner be *taught* in a classroom, any more than human beings rely on 'teachers' to acquire mastery of their first language. Indeed, much of the significant learning we do in life, and much of the significant language learning which individuals, for a variety of reasons, undertake at different stages of their lives, occur outside classroom walls unassisted – some would state unencumbered – by a 'classroom teacher'.

It is important to state at the outset that Dickinson's focus in the main is the adult learner. The principles outlined here are equally valid for school-aged language learners, but they tend to be ignored by teachers in favour of instructional designs which foster classroom learning. As more and more adults, no longer enrolled in educational institutions, find it necessary or desirable to learn a new language for personal or professional reasons, the technology of self-instruction will continue to gain in importance. Dickinson considers such issues as individual preparation for self-instruction, materials for self-instruction, and ways of engaging in self-assessment. This is very much a language teachers' book, for there is considerable information about the design and execution of self-instruction which can be implemented beneficially in the school context. The book is also relevant to individuals planning to undertake a language learning experience on their own. I have found this book extremely helpful to me in shaping my thinking on these issues. I recommend it highly to all those who care about the quality of language learning – their own, or that of others.

Howard B. Altman
University of Louisville
Kentucky, USA

Introduction

There are many ways to set about writing a book such as this, and one of the ways I have *not* adopted is to base the book on the results of research showing the effectiveness of self-instruction in language learning: the results do not exist because the research has not been done. But then, very few of the present or past methods and techniques for language learning are solidly based on research results. Either the research has not been done for them or the results are inconclusive.

Where I know of relevant research results on the effectiveness of self-instruction, I have referred to them: otherwise, I have tried to make it clear that the procedures and techniques recommended here are suggestions and speculations. Finally, the book might make a small contribution to research by offering a number of hypotheses that could be tested.

Sometimes we language teachers adopt methods and techniques because they are in vogue, but mostly we adopt them because their aims and their view of language learning seem sensible and appealing. The kind of self-instruction described in this book seems sensible to me and I am offering it on that basis. It seems sensible to organise language learning classrooms in such a way that individual needs, interests and preferred learning strategies can be catered for. It seems sensible for institutions to consider the needs of learners who cannot attend classes regularly in college time. It also seems sensible for teachers to teach.

A naive view of self-instruction is one in which the teacher is seen as redundant. There is no likelihood of this happening, for there are many occasions on which the teacher is called upon to teach in a self-instructional mode. On other occasions the teacher has a vital role, but it is different from that traditionally accorded to the teacher. What this book is about, then, is ways of introducing greater flexibility into institutions and into language learning classrooms, so that, for example, teachers teach only part of the time, and the remaining time is devoted to facilitating learning in other ways; so that learners with special needs, whether in terms of aptitude, purposes, or in terms of their own availability, can be catered for; and so that every learner's right to self-direction is respected.

However, it is necessary to inject a note of caution. Only a few people are spontaneously self-directed. Many turn to self-instruction as a solution to an otherwise intractable problem – for example, an inability to get to classes because of family or job responsibilities, or because their language learning objectives would not be met in the course available. It is not desirable to thrust self-instruction and self-directed learning on to learners who are resistant to it, and it is very important that those of us who are enthusiastic about self-instruction do not confuse the idea, or our enthusiasm to introduce it, with the learner's ability or willingness to undertake it. I believe that the way forward is to introduce into the learning programme elements which train learners towards greater autonomy and aim towards a gradual development to full autonomy. Such an approach is particularly important at the school level.

Language teaching and learning have frequently been beset by techniques in which the tail wags the dog. Thus the language laboratory – essentially a useful technique – became a controlling factor in some methodologies, so that language learning and teaching was organised around the language laboratory. Self-instruction and self-directed learning may pose a similar threat of a particular learning mode taking over the whole of the learning programme and distorting it so that the covert aim becomes the success of self-directed learning rather than the successful learning of the target language. Self-instruction must be judged by its effectiveness as a learning mode – that is, it must be judged by the success of learners in learning the foreign language.

Of course, I believe that self-direction is different in kind from simple techniques like language laboratories or micro-computers, and I believe that learners should strive towards autonomy in learning. But autonomy is an ultimate; it constitutes a kind of Nirvana to be achieved through struggle. Learners do not achieve autonomy by being told to, nor by being denied conventional class teaching; in these ways they are likely only to achieve failure. Autonomy is achieved slowly, through struggling towards it, through careful training and careful preparation on the teacher's part as well as on the learner's, and the first stage in this process is the liberalisation of the classroom to allow the development of learner independence and learner responsibility.

Much of this book is concerned with procedures and techniques for achieving this greater flexibility in the language classroom, and many of the procedures and techniques suggested have been suggested and developed by other teachers. I am indebted to all these people, for without them the book would not exist. I am greatly indebted to past and present members of the Centre de Recherches et d'Applications Pédagogiques en Langues (CRAPEL) of the University of Nancy II, France, especially Henri Holec, Harvey Moulden and Philip Riley. I am particularly grateful to colleagues in my own institution, the Scottish Centre for Education Overseas in Moray House College of Education, Edinburgh, especially David Carver and Bill Cousin. Amongst many others who have helped me in various ways are James McCafferty of the British Council and Ray Mackay. Desmond O'Sullivan, my editor, has been tremendously helpful and supportive. The person to whom I owe most is Norma Dickinson, my wife, and a colleague, with whom I have had many spirited discussions on self-directed learning, and who is both the source of many of the ideas in the book, and my most severe critic.

Part I
Basic issues in self-instruction: introduction

Self-instruction for many people conjures up visions of a learner, totally on his own, rehearsing irregular verbs from a published course with a title something like *Personalised Instruction in French*. This certainly is one possible example of self-instruction but it is by no means the only one. A pupil in a secondary school French class may also be involved in self-instruction for part of his time. Indeed, self-instruction in the form of homework has a long history.

It is the purpose of Chapter 1 to set out the possibilities that the term self-instruction describes and to attempt to sort out the terminology that has grown up recently around this area – terms like autonomy, self-directed learning, self-access and individualisation.

Chapter 2 begins by pointing out that simply demonstrating that something is possible is not a justification for adopting it. That self-instruction is possible is shown in Chapter 1 but the question 'why use self-instruction?' still needs an answer. Chapter 2 marshals several arguments in favour of some degree of self-instruction: these range from reasons of practical convenience to the ideological desirability of promoting autonomy as a general outcome of education. The intention of this part of the book, then, is to persuade the reader that self-instruction is both viable and desirable as a mode of learning.

1 What is self-instruction?

The label 'self-instruction' is used to refer to situations in which a learner, with others, or alone, is working without the direct control of a teacher. This might be for short periods within a lesson, for whole lessons, or in the extreme case of learner autonomy, where he* undertakes the whole of his learning without the help of a teacher. This chapter begins with a number of 'case studies' which illustrate several of the possibilities of self-instruction. In order to categorise the different types, a basic distinction is made between *learner-centred* and *materials-centred* self-instruction, the former being characterised by modes which place responsibility on the learner while the latter builds the teacher's role into the teaching materials. On the basis of this distinction the chapter defines some of the terms which are used to label self-instructional learning modes commonly used in the professional literature. Finally, the possibilities for self-instruction are presented in a diagram which is then discussed in the text.

1.1 Some examples

Example 1 David Maxwell

> David Maxwell is sixteen years old and is at secondary school. His French classes would be familiar enough to most language teachers. His teacher uses the course book selected by the Modern Languages department in the school; the teacher presents the new material to the class, gets the class, either all together or in groups, to practise it in various ways, and she devises ways in which the pupils can use the new language. In addition, every week David, as well as the other pupils in the class, is asked to think about the reading he is going to do in French for the next week. The library in the school has a good selection of books in French, ranging from simple, sometimes simplified, stories to full novels and non-fiction books on a range

* Since teachers and learners include both males and females it is important that both personal pronouns should be used. The easiest way to ensure equitable treatment is to alternate 'she' and 'he' and their variants by chapter. Thus 'he' is used in this chapter, 'she' in the next, and so on throughout the book.

of topics. Each pupil in David's class is expected to do some reading in French each week, though what an individual does depends on that person's ability in French and his interests. By now the pupils are in the habit of going to the library some time during the week to select their reading material, although junior classes are taken there by the teacher. Once David has made his selection, he enters it on a 'contract' form, which involves writing in the title and author, and a very brief note on why he has selected that particular book. This might simply be something like 'It looks an interesting story' or 'I enjoyed the last story I read by this author.' Or it might indicate a wider learning project a pupil is incidentally involved in – 'I'm interested in French cooking.' In addition to this information, David has to decide approximately how much of the book – how many pages – he will read during the week. Finally he writes a note on how he is going to demonstrate that he has achieved what he set out to do. If he undertakes to read a story for pleasure, he may decide to write a brief account of it in English – or maybe a briefer one in French. If he is engaged in reading a book on cooking he may decide to make notes on recipes and to build up a specialised vocabulary of cooking terms. The teacher checks the contracts at intervals and looks at a sample of pupils' written work each week. When a pupil decides to write an account in French, it is understood between the class and the teacher that he takes the account to the teacher for checking.

In David's case, then, self-instruction is only a small part of his total French instruction, and there is relatively close supervision by the teacher. The self-instructional aspect of Dr Cornelius's learning is also only part of the total instruction, but in her case it is self-initiated.

Example 2 Dr Cornelius

Dr Cornelius is a lecturer in microbiology at the university. She is an experienced language learner, having learned French, Russian and German in the past, and speaking and reading them fluently. She is very fond of Italy and things Italian, and for the past two years has gone to Italy with her children on camping holidays. She decides to learn Italian and so joins a class at a local College of Further Education. In her experience of language learning, the most difficult and least pleasant phase is the initial period of gaining command over the basic grammar and pronunciation. Consequently, she believes in studying as intensively as possible for the first six months or so. The only available class meets twice a week for two hours at each meeting, so if she is to study more intensively she must do so herself. Using the resources of the college library, and the university library, and taking advice from

> the teacher, she collects all the material she can in Italian. She listens to Italian recordings, struggles through Italian newspapers using a dictionary and a grammar, and, drawing on her knowledge of Latin and other languages, she learns chunks of the grammar, and keeps a vocabulary list.

Dr Cornelius's involvement in self-instruction is different in several respects from David Maxwell's, but they are similar in that both are following a taught course. However, Dr Cornelius has deliberately chosen to join a class as part of the instructional package she has designed for herself, and the self-instructional elements are also self-initiated and self-designed. In this respect Liz Pearson's case is similar.

Example 3 Liz Pearson

> Liz Pearson wishes to become a bilingual secretary in English and French. She attends classes at the French Institute in her home city, to build on the French she learned at school. The class she attends is concerned with improving general reading, writing, and speaking skills. Liz Pearson recognises that in addition to this common core language she requires more specialist language skills in order to perform the tasks of a bilingual secretary. In particular she needs to be able to read and reply to letters in the target language, to answer the telephone and deal with semi-technical enquiries, and to undertake a small amount of translation and interpretation. She, therefore, approaches the teacher at the French Institute and discusses her needs. The teacher is sympathetic, but not very knowledgeable in this particular area of French for specific purposes; however the teacher is able to help in two ways. She helps Liz Pearson to select one or two possible course books from the library, and she introduces her to the secretary in the Institute who is a native speaker of French, and who is of course a bilingual secretary. Through her, Liz Pearson is able to construct a supplementary programme of study relevant to her ambitions.

Adrian Chapman, however, is different. He has decided not to join a class, but he makes use of several other language learning opportunities available in his area.

Example 4 Adrian Chapman

> Adrian Chapman learned some French in school ten years ago, but now has forgotten it. He intends to go to France on holiday in a year's time and so wishes to learn the language. In addition he thinks that his job opportunities (he works in a bank) will be enhanced if he knows a European language. For various reasons he is unwilling to give up two evenings a week to attend evening

> classes, so he follows the BBC beginners' French course *Ensemble*. In addition he discovers that the local College of Further Education has a 'Learning by Appointment Scheme' where, for a small fee, people can book a language laboratory booth and use a selection of course materials to further their studies. He also discovers that the college administers a 'learning exchange scheme' in which individuals offer to teach others various skills. He contacts someone who offers French conversation, and is able to get this person to check his pronunciation, help him with simple sentences and so on.

All of these people are involved in self-instruction of one kind or another, but it is clear that there is a range of possibilities covered by this term. What is common throughout the range is the notion of learner responsibility.

Self-instruction is concerned with responsibility in learning. Individuals who are involved in self-instruction (as learners) have undertaken some additional responsibility for their own learning which in other circumstances would be held on their behalf by a teacher. Clearly, people can be involved in self-instruction to various degrees. For some it may be total, so that no teacher is involved at all; for others – the more likely situation – self-instruction will be part of a package involving both conventional teaching and self-instruction.

Similarly, people may adopt self-instruction (either partial or total) for various reasons. For the individual adult learner the reasons are likely to be either practical or a matter of the preferred manner of learning. Practical reasons include such things as the learner being unable, conveniently, to attend classes regularly or at all, or else the learner's needs are such that no class is offered which meets them, and so on. The adoption of total self-instruction solely because it is the preferred manner of learning is likely to be relatively rare, though many learners must adopt it as the best option when there are no classes, or they are held at inconvenient times, or at some considerable distance from the learner's home. Partial self-instruction, on the other hand, is a very common device adopted by learners and suggested by teachers to supplement a taught course in various ways.

1.2 Terminology and definitions

The term self-instruction is one among many possible labels for this kind of approach to learning. I will use it as a general cover term to make broad reference to situations in which learners are working without the direct control of a teacher. Other terms, however, need to be more carefully defined. There are numerous terms used in the literature of self-instruction and the number has tended to increase as interest in the area has grown: here, however, I will be concerned only with the five most commonly encountered. These are autonomy, semi-autonomy, individualised instruction, (including individualisation), self-directed learning and self-access learning (and self-access materials).

1.2.1 Responsibility for learning

The main key to understanding this terminology concerns the concept of responsibility for learning and wherein the responsibility lies. The act of learning something must always be a personal, individual act. No-one can learn the meaning of a word for me, though, of course, others can help me towards that end. In language learning, the learning that individuals achieve results from a complex organisation of materials, lessons, drills, exercises, tests and so on. Traditionally, the teacher is responsible for setting up this organisation and for managing it in the classroom. Allwright (1978) has noted that the teacher is responsible for a daunting list of management tasks, and suggests that the responsibility for at least some of them might be shared with learners. The tasks he notes include such things as determining learning goals, making decisions about materials, deciding how the materials will be used, keeping records, evaluating progress, allocating time to tasks, deciding on what tasks will be done, and who should do them, what groupings the learners will work in and so on. (See the introduction to Part II.)

One view of self-instruction is that in which the teacher seeks to include the learners increasingly in this decision-making process about their learning and the management of it; the teacher seeks to transfer to the learners an increasing degree of responsibility for their own learning. In this view, an autonomous learner is one who is totally responsible for making and implementing all of the decisions concerned with his own learning.

An opposing view is one in which the materials and resources for learning are written and organised in such a way that the decision making and much of the management of the learning are built into the materials. (Early forms of programmed learning, in particular linear programmes, were an extreme example of this.) In this view, the learners' responsibility may be limited to matters concerning when the work takes place, and perhaps which parts of the programme to work on at particular times.

These two views are not placed in an 'either/or' opposition, but are at opposite ends of a continuum. Using this concept of responsibility for learning, we can make an initial sorting of the terms. A diagrammatic representation might help to clarify the relationships. (See figure 1.)

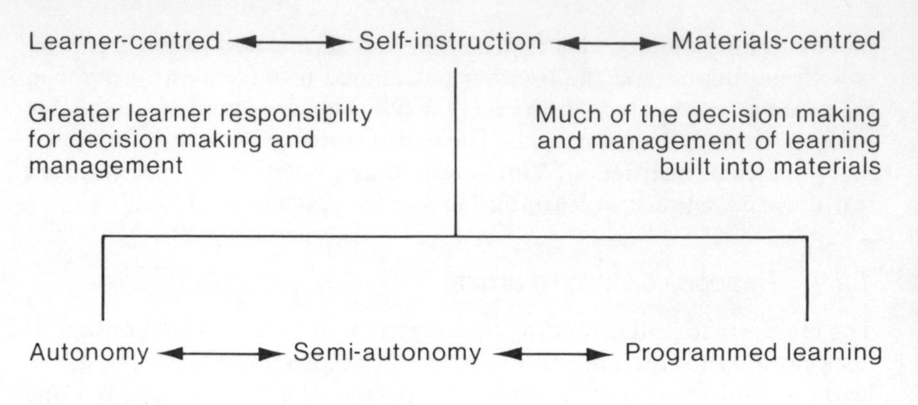

Figure 1

Three of the terms do not appear on this diagram: self-direction does not easily fit in because it is concerned with the learner's responsibility for making the decisions about his learning, but does not entail the learner undertaking the implementation (or management) of the decisions. The relationship between autonomy and self-direction will be discussed shortly.

Both 'self-access' and individualised instruction are used in many different ways, and to place them on this diagram would involve choosing one possible use among many and this would misrepresent the situation. The term self-access is often used as though it was a method or technique; it is, of course, neither. Self-access refers to the organisation of learning materials (and possibly equipment) to make them directly available to the learner. Making learning materials directly available to the learner raises a wide range of questions relating to how this is done; how this way of learning is related to the principal method; questions relating to the learner and his ability to take advantage of materials; questions about the learner's ability to identify his learning needs, his ability to match his needs with appropriate materials; techniques for enabling him to do so, and his ability to use the materials effectively. And finally, it raises questions about the appropriateness of the materials for self-instruction, how such appropriateness is judged, and how inappropriate materials can be modified and supplemented. These are all questions with which this book is concerned, and they will be thoroughly examined in Part II.

Individualised instruction is used, by different writers, in ways that place it at both ends of the scale of responsibility for learning. That is, some authors use it to describe situations where the learners are provided with specially prepared materials into which are built many of the management controls usually operated by the teacher. Others use individualised instruction to describe learning situations for which I would use the terms self-directed learning or autonomous learning. Though individualisation is concerned with the individual differences of the learners it may not offer very much independence to the learner. An individualised course in which each learner is directed to a particular level by the teacher, where the students' learning needs are anticipated, perhaps even determined, by the material, and which is worked on during the appropriate timetabled hours does not leave much freedom for independent learning by the learner. The term is, however, used by other authors to label autonomous or semi-autonomous learning.

1.2.2 Summary of definitions

- *Self-instruction.* This is a neutral term referring generally to situations in which learners are working without the direct control of the teacher.
- *Self-direction.* This term describes a particular attitude to the learning task, where the learner accepts responsibility for all the decisions concerned with his learning but does not necessarily undertake the implementation of those decisions.
- *Autonomy.* This term describes the situation in which the learner is totally responsible for all of the decisions concerned with his learning and the implementation of those decisions. In full autonomy there is no involvement of a 'teacher' or an institution. And the learner is also independent of specially prepared materials.
- *Semi-autonomy.* This conveniently labels the stage at which learners are preparing for autonomy.
- *Self-access materials.* These are materials appropriate to and available for self-instruction.
- *Self-access learning.* This is self-instruction using these materials. The term is neutral as to how self-directed or other-directed the learners are.
- *Individualised instruction.* Once again this term is neutral as to who takes the responsibility for the learning. Chaix and O'Neil (1978) define it as: 'a learning process which (as regards goals content, methodology and pacing) is adapted to a particular individual, taking this individual's characteristics into consideration'.

The term *self-direction* is different from the others in the list in that it refers to attitudes rather than techniques or even modes of instruction. Self-access learning, or individualised instruction, for example, refer to *modes of learning* in that they are concerned with the activities of the learner, the teacher and their interaction. Self-directed learning, in contrast, describes an attitude to learning in which the learner accepts responsibility for his learning, but he does not necessarily carry out courses of action independently in connection with it. Consequently, a learner may be self-directed and yet following a conventional teacher-led class; similarly a self-directed learner may follow any one of the possible self-instructional modes. Indeed in this latter case, the chances of success are greatly enhanced if the learner *is* self-directed; and if the self-instructional mode is learner-centred, then self-direction is a requirement for success.

1.2.3 Self-direction

Self-direction, then, is a second key to understanding self-instruction. But what does it mean to be self-directed? What does it mean to take responsibility for one's own learning? Self-direction refers to a particular attitude towards learning, one in which (as I have said above) the learner is prepared to take responsibility for his own learning. This idea frequently strikes teachers as impossibly idealistic and unrealistic, so it is worth examining it in detail. In fact, outside of the context of education, we take responsibility for a whole range of things, many of which we know little about. The first point to be made about this, then, is to distinguish between being responsible for something, and carrying out courses of action arising from that responsibility. To be responsible for something does not entail having to carry out the courses of action arising from it.

For example, as a parent I am responsible for my children's health, but that does not mean that I must undertake the diagnosis and treatment of their illnesses. The expression of my responsibility in this area is to make decisions about when to seek expert help, and what kind of expert help to seek. But even at this point I do not abandon responsibility: I wish to know what the diagnosis is, what treatment is proposed, what the implications of the treatment are (and if these are unacceptable, what alternatives there are), how long the treatment is likely to take, and what the prognosis is. A good doctor will expect to provide such information and will welcome the parents' concern.

Another example of responsibility is for the house in which I live. I am responsible for maintaining it in good order, and ensuring that the roof does not leak, or the pipes freeze, or the woodwork go rotten and so on. I have a number of choices about how to carry out this responsibility. I can do everything myself, or I can call in expert help; or, I can combine the two – do the checking myself and get expert help to do the work.

The situation is similar with respect to self-directed learning. The self-directed learner retains responsibility for all aspects of the management of his learning but will probably seek expert help and advice for many of these. Even those learning in conventional classes with highly directive teachers can retain responsibility for their own learning in this sense, although their scope for assisting with the management of their learning will be greatly curtailed.

A self-directed learner, then, is one who retains responsibility for the management of his own learning. If the learner, in addition, undertakes all these management tasks himself, then he is also autonomous, that is, he no longer requires help from a teacher to organise his learning. However, it is worth noting here that many autonomous learners work with others in their learning – autonomy does not imply isolation.

1.2.4 Degrees of autonomy

Once again there are numerous degrees of self-direction, and various levels of autonomy. Just as I suggested earlier that there was a scale of the focus of responsibility of learning, so here we can recognise a scale of degree of autonomy. We need to recognise such a scale if we are to represent accurately the reality of language learning inside and out of educational institutions.

The learners in the examples given earlier can be regarded as self-directed in that they retain responsibility for some of their learning. Only Adrian Chapman, however, can be regarded as autonomous*. We could describe two of the others as semi-autonomous. Both Liz Pearson and Dr Cornelius have decided to tackle one part of their language learning needs through taking a course, and they have supplemented the course with other work they have selected. The fourth case, David Maxwell, is being prepared for greater autonomy in his learning by being given responsibility for part of it.

It is clear from these examples that there is not a simple dichotomy between autonomous language learning and fully directed language learning, but that there are a vast range of possibilities between these extremes. The diagram in figure 2 attempts to indicate the range of these options.

Each of the columns indicates a range of possibilities from a high degree of external direction (at the foot of the column) to full autonomy at the top. The possibility of movement from a more externally directed to a more autonomous learning style (and vice versa) is shown by an instruction to move up or down to a numbered node-point. Thus, in the column labelled Materials, an individual – like David Maxwell in example 1 – who is learning within a conventional classroom, and who consequently is not free to make all the decisions concerned with his learning, might be offered a degree of freedom to select from a range of materials for part of his learning, indicated in the diagram by an instruc-

* Though he is not fully autonomous in that he is using prepared materials for learning.

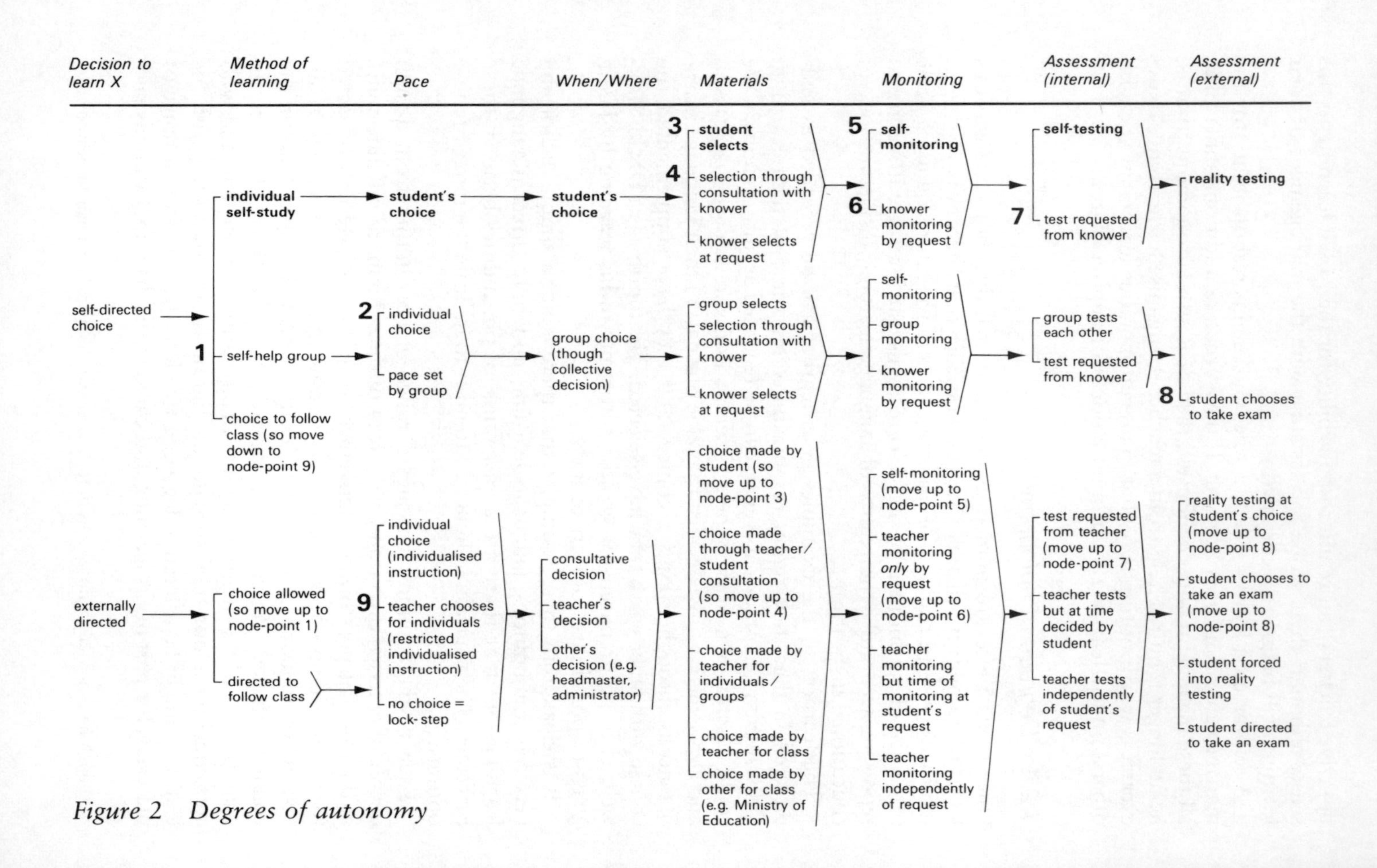

Figure 2 Degrees of autonomy

tion to 'move up to node-point 3'. Such a choice would be offered, for example, in an individualised learning scheme.

Similarly, an individual who has made a free choice to study a language may choose to join a class for the whole or part of that study – as was the case with the examples of Liz Pearson and Dr Cornelius. This is indicated in the column labelled Method of learning by the instruction 'move down to node-point 9'. The top line across this diagram indicates the route taken by a fully autonomous learner.

The promotion of self-direction encourages learners to make free choices, including the choice to follow a highly directed course. Self-instruction is where the learner undertakes parts, or all, of the instructional tasks, represented in the upper part of the diagram. Autonomy is where the learner takes responsibility for his learning and undertakes all of the management tasks concerned with it. In making this distinction, we are departing from the way these terms are used by other educationalists. Knowles (1975: 18), for example, uses the term self-direction to mean the same as self-instruction – as well as self-planned learning, self-education, self-teaching, self-study and autonomous learning. Holec (1980: 5) makes the same distinction as that made here, but reverses the terms so that for him autonomy describes an attitude and self-direction a mode of learning. There is no need to invest a lot of effort in attempting to disentangle these terms here. The important point is the distinction between an attitude to the learning process which recognises the learner's responsibility in learning, and a mode of learning – most conveniently called self-instruction – in which the learner takes over part, or all, of the instructional process without the direct intervention of the teacher.

1.3 An overview of the book

It is clear that learners are more likely to make use of a self-instructional mode of learning firstly if they are self-directed, and secondly if the learning environment is organised in such a way as to facilitate self-instruction. The preparation of learners for self-direction is achieved, to a large extent, through giving them explicit opportunities to regain responsibility for their own learning. With adults it may be sufficient simply to make alternative options available, together with opportunities to learn about self-instructional techniques. Indeed with adults there is rarely time for a leisurely programme of preparation for self-direction, since they usually have pressing needs to acquire the language they are setting out to learn. Ways of preparing adults for self-instruction are described mainly in Chapter 7. With children it is both necessary and possible to develop self-direction during school education. The approach recommended in this book is to use those conventional instructional techniques which offer learners a greater degree of responsibility for their own learning and greater independence in the process. Obvious devices such as group work and project work offer these possibilities as do less common devices such as pupil record keeping and self-assessment. The crucial issues for the teacher in all of this are what can he or she actually do, and what materials can be used to do it! These matters are dealt with in the second part of the book; this is called *Facilitating learning* and attempts to describe possible structures and their components within which self-instruction is possible. In addition, the final chapter is concerned with self-assessment. The view held in this book is that an essential ingredient in undertaking responsibility for one's own learning is judging whether or not it has been successful.

Self-assessment, then, is a vital part of self-instruction. Of course, there are times when learners will wish to present themselves for external assessment, most commonly when they are seeking certification of their learning. There is no necessary conflict between self-assessment and external assessment for certification; the two can be happily accommodated in a self-instructional system. Any learner who wishes to gain a qualification offered by some agency must accept the terms on which the agency offers the qualification. That is they must pass the assessment requirements. Self-direction can be expressed in such matters as when and how to prepare for the assessments, and often, when to take a particular examination. Similarly, any agency offering a qualification in any subject whatever has the responsibility of specifying what the candidate is required to do, and what standard he is required to reach to gain the qualification. Occasionally, an agency will invite candidates to specify how they propose to demonstrate that they have reached the appropriate proficiency in the relevant subject. However, this does not, nor cannot mean that the agency will accept any standard whatever; under these circumstances, the certification would be meaningless. The agency establishes its standards, and checks proposals against that standard. A useful example is the way the Doctor of Philosophy degree is awarded in British universities. The candidate proposes a topic and then submits a dissertation on the topic. The university judges the acceptability of the topic and assures itself that the standard reached is appropriate, but the choice of topic, and how competence is to be demonstrated, is left to the candidate.

1.4 Conclusion

Self-instruction may mean a learner working away in isolation, but it is more likely to describe a situation in which learners undertake responsibility for a part of their learning. Also, it may mean a learner using materials which are designed to guide his every step and leave little freedom of choice, or it may describe a situation in which the learner designs his own course and makes decisions about when and how he is going to be assessed. Finally, it is true to say that because a particular instructional mode is possible does not mean that it is desirable. The question, expressed boldly as 'why bother?', or more cautiously as 'what are the justifications for self-instruction?' is an essential one to be answered, and this is the topic of the next chapter.

2 Why self-instruction?

Facilitating self-instruction, as readers will see from Part II, involves teachers in a considerable amount of preparatory work, and involves both learners and teachers in learning new techniques of instruction and in adjusting their accustomed roles. Furthermore, as with much innovation in education, there are many risks of things going wrong. Why then is self-instruction recommended? There are five main reasons and several minor ones. These are summarised in figure 3.

2.1 Practical reasons

The most obvious justification for self-instruction is that there are circumstances where there is no alternative, or where any alternative involves the learner in unacceptable personal sacrifice. Thus the learner may live at a considerable distance from an appropriate institution; the learner's job may not allow her the free time, or the time at the right part of the week, to attend classes (people on shift work, working overtime etc.); or the learner may be disabled and unable to attend classes. The learner's language learning needs may not fit with the available courses in various ways; the learner may require a particular competence in a relatively short time, so needing an intensive course, but the only available course, or perhaps the only one the learner can *afford*, lasts two years at two hours per week. The learner may need to learn bits of the language which are underemphasised, or not touched upon, by most courses. (A glance through lists of books on English for Specific Purposes suggests that there are quite a lot of learners with specialist needs.) But sometimes the needs are not all that special – just different from those emphasised by the course. There must be many people who want to learn a foreign language primarily for reading but find that the only available course insists, for whatever reason, on emphasising aural/oral skills.

2.2 Individual differences among learners

The second reason for advocating self-instruction is that it is a way of coping with the various sorts of differences among learners. The import-

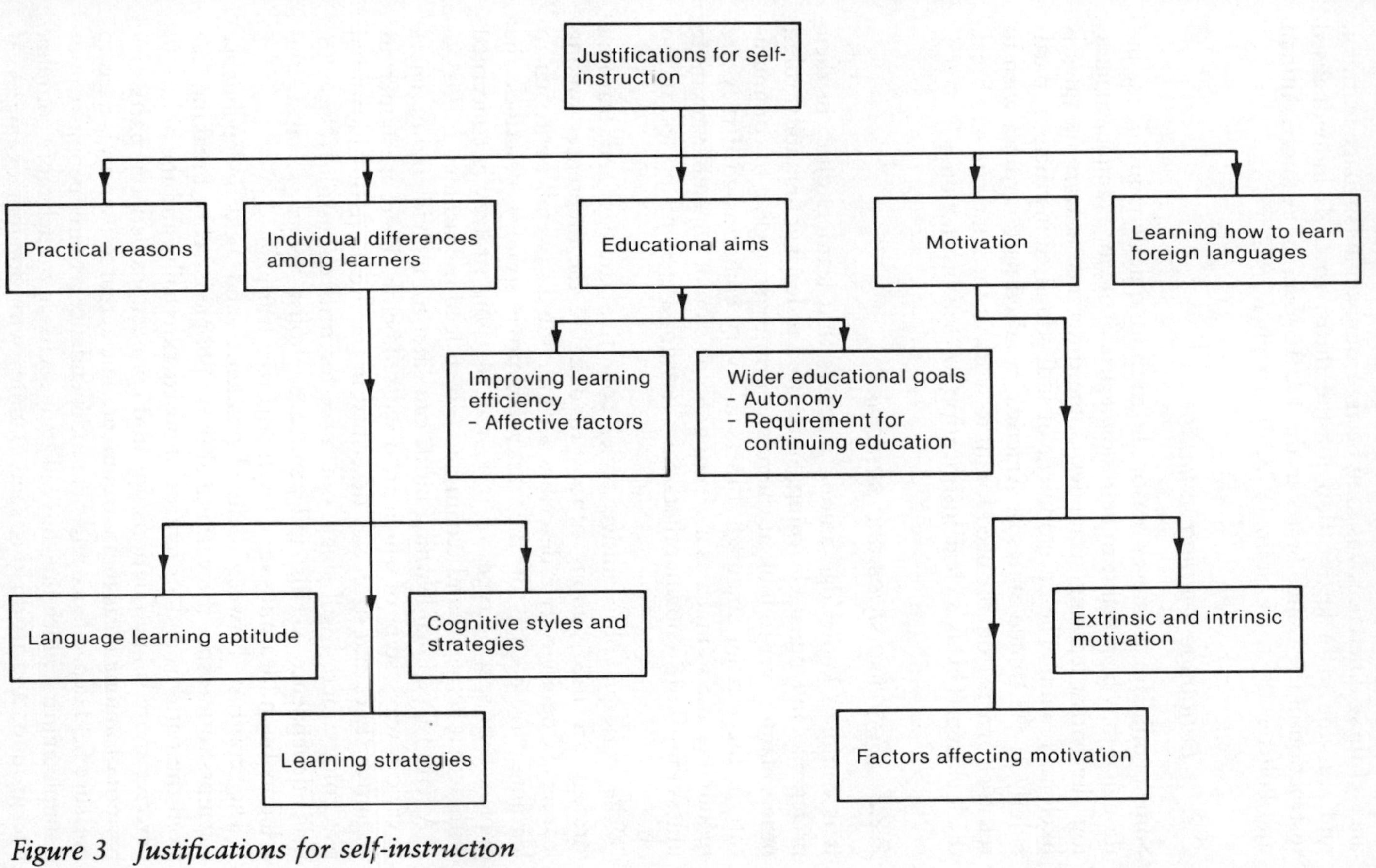

Figure 3 Justifications for self-instruction

ance of these differences has long been recognised in language learning, and was the main justification for the thrust towards individualised instruction in the United States in the 1970s. (See, for example, Altman and Politzer 1971, Chastain 1975, or Gougher 1972.)

2.2.1 Language learning aptitude

Some people, for whatever reason, learn more quickly than others, and though it may be possible to help slow learners by, for example, suggesting alternative learning strategies, some difference in learning rates is likely to remain. The development of individualised instruction, particularly in the United States of America, resulted partly from a wish to release learners from the need for all to work at the same rate – to break the lockstep. This is a clear justification for self-instruction.

2.2.2 Cognitive styles and strategies

It is common knowledge among teachers that learners differ in their preferences in language learning. Some need to learn grammatical rules, others claim never to look at them; some enjoy struggling to communicate in the foreign language, others are very embarrassed if they are required to use so much as a greeting. Some cannot remember anything unless they write it down, others have very good aural memories, and so on.

The concepts of cognitive style, cognitive strategy and learning strategy are used, among others, to describe the differences among learners. Cognitive style describes an individual's overall approach to learning, irrespective of the task; cognitive strategy describes the approach to specific types of task, and learning strategy is concerned with actual activities and techniques which lead to learning.

A self-instructional learning mode can cater for individual differences in various ways, some of which are discussed below. There are numerous cognitive styles and strategies described in the literature of educational psychology; here I will single out three for brief discussion. These are field dependence versus independence; holist versus serialist and syllabus-bound learning versus syllabus-free learning.

The contrast between field dependence and field independence attempts to measure the varying abilities people have for breaking free from the patterns and structures imposed externally, and the ability to perceive more subtle relationships and connections between parts of a pattern or among ideas in an argument. The actual test which is used to measure field dependence and field independence requires people to spot a simple figure – which they have already seen – in a much more complex background, and to do this several times with different examples. If people are successful in the test, it is presumed that they can transfer this ability to many rather different mental tasks which involve identifying, or maybe creating, alternative patterns within a whole structure. Such people – field independents – are presumed to have the ability to impose structure on a learning task by extracting general principles; they acquire new concepts after several trials by a flash of insight. Field dependents, on the other hand, tend to work from each example in a sequence in turn rather than looking for, or creating, overall generalisations, and this step-by-step approach results in learning which shows gradual improvement (Wilson 1981:139). There is little research on the relationship between field dependence/independence and language learning, so we can only speculate on what might be the case. Since field dependents prefer a step-by-step approach then they may favour language learning materials which are carefully graded, such as structural drills and exercises. On the other hand, field independents may prefer more global activities. Two implications may follow: firstly it is desirable to have a learning mode which favours these kinds of learning activities; and secondly it may be necessary to offer guidance to learners who show an extreme inclination in either direction. Thus field dependents may need to be guided to more global activities and field independents to drill and exercise activities concerned with accuracy. (Harding-Esch 1976b originated this suggestion with reference to serialists and holists, discussed below.)

The distinction between holist and serialist learning has some apparent relationships with field independence/dependence. According to Entwistle (1981) holist learners tend to ask questions about broad relations and form hypotheses about generalisations, while serialists ask questions about much narrower relations and form specific hypotheses. Entwistle (1981) describes tests devised by Pask (the originator of the distinction) which are based on real learning tasks. Students were identified as either serialist or holist learners and were then asked to work through learning materials and to take a test to see how much they had learned. There were two sets of materials, one designed to suit holists and the other designed to suit serialists. However, some students were deliberately given the 'wrong' materials – that is materials designed for holists were given to serialists and vice versa. 'The results were dramatic ... The students in the matched condition were able to answer most of the questions about what they had learned whereas the other students generally fell to below half marks.' (Entwistle 1981:95)

Once again, in the absence of research relevant to language learning, we can only speculate on the implications. As with field independents and dependents, it may be the case that serialists will be attracted to the step-by-step procedures required by drills and similar activities, while holists will be happier with activities concerned with language use. If

Pask's findings on the importance of the match between learner type and materials type are valid for language learning, then this is another justification for a system which 'breaks the lockstep', but this time a lockstep of everyone using the same materials.

The distinction between syllabus-bound learners (sylbs) and syllabus-free learners (sylfs) is largely a matter of the needs of different individuals for externally imposed structure on their study. Sylbs claim to study only what they are required to study, whilst sylfs may find the syllabus restrictive; they claim often to be involved in following up their own ideas when they are supposed to be doing homework. They have a wide range of outside interests which are absorbing and conflict with the demands of the set work (Wilson 1981:145).

It is arguable that to be a successful language learner beyond the elementary stages – as characterised by judgements of communicative fluency rather than by test and examination results – it is necessary to become free of externally imposed syllabuses. A language course can provide the basic grammatical structure and initial vocabulary, can indicate the sound system and pronunciation, can offer a degree of grading and suggestions for practice, but as soon as learners begin to take off in the language it is likely that their demand for interesting content will take them beyond the confines of any course or syllabus. Even at the elementary levels, learners need to supplement the course materials with extra reading and listening materials, or find other ways of immersing themselves in the language. Naiman *et al.* (1978) and Pickett (1978) conducted surveys among good language learners asking them about their own approach to learning a language. The self-reports from these surveys tend to confirm that good learners are more likely to show the characteristics of sylfs rather than sylbs.

2.2.3 Learning strategies

All learners manifest certain preferred learning strategies – particular forms of observable behaviour, more or less consciously employed by the learner (Stern 1983:409). Learning strategies include, for example, strategies for coping with target language rules, including such devices as generalisation and simplification; strategies for receiving performance, and for producing performance. (See Carver 1984 for a comprehensive list of learning strategies.) Each of these distinctions in cognitive style, strategy and learning techniques suggests that any group of learners will manifest several differences in the preferred ways of going about learning tasks, and that learning is unlikely to be most efficient if the learner is prevented from learning in the ways she prefers. However, it may be possible, through a course of preparation, to persuade the learner to use more effective strategies (see Chapter 7). This argues for a flexible approach to the provision of learning facilities, and one aspect of this flexibility is to provide facilities for self-instruction as it is defined in Chapter 1.

2.3 Educational aims

This section divides broadly into two: a part concerned with learning efficiency, and one concerned with wider educational goals such as the promotion of autonomy, and the facilitation of continuing education.

2.3.1 Improving learning efficiency

Learning efficiency is likely to be related to many different kinds of factors, some of them relatively stable characteristics of the individual and others responsive to changes in the learning mode, changes in attitude and so on. Stern (1983:411) hypothesises that good learners are likely to exhibit four basic sets of strategies:

- *An active planning strategy*. Good language learners have the ability to select goals and sub-goals and recognise stages and developmental sequences.
- *An academic (explicit) learning strategy*. Good language learners are able to view a language as a formal system with rules and regular relationships between language forms and meanings. They analyse the language and develop the necessary techniques of practice and memorisation. They monitor their own performance and revise it in order to progress towards an improved second language command.
- *A social learning strategy*. Good language learners recognise that in the early stages of learning they will have a dependent status in the target language, and they are able to accept the resultant role as a linguistic infant. They seek communicative contact with target language users and the target language community; they develop techniques of coping with difficulties in the language. They become actively involved as participants in authentic language use.
- *An effective strategy*. Good language learners cope effectively with the emotional and motivational problems of language learning. In spite of the difficulties of language and culture shock they cultivate positive attitudes towards themselves as language learners, towards language and language learning in general, and towards the target language, its society and culture.

Self-instruction helps learners to develop the first two strategies. In addition, self-instruction supports learners in their development of social learning strategies and in coping with the emotional and motivational problems of language learning. Self-instruction helps learners to acquire the first two strategies by encouraging them to take on greater responsibility for their own learning. Thus learners are encouraged to consider their own learning needs, and in some cases to undertake a substantial analysis of them. In this way, the learners become aware of possible goals, stages and sequences in language learning. They are encouraged to select relevant goals and sub-goals at which to aim, and to monitor and assess their achievements through various self-assessment techniques. This process may be conceptualised as learning how to learn language, and is discussed in 2.5, in Chapter 7 and in Carver and Dickinson (1982a) and Dickinson and Carver (1980).

Self-instruction seeks to give to the learner as much responsibility for her learning as she can cope with at any particular time. Where a learner achieves self-direction then she accepts responsibility in four areas:

- The self-directed learner retains responsibility for the aims and objectives of the course. This may simply mean that she is aware of them and accepts them.
- She monitors the development of the course and its continuing relevance to her own objectives. This may be a course presented by a teacher in a conventional classroom setting, it may be a course of study individually tailored to the learner and undertaken in a self-instructional mode, or it may be a combination of the two.
- The self-directed learner assesses herself. This entails, as a minimum, that she is aware of how well she achieves learning tasks, and has a reasonable idea of her level of proficiency.
- The self-directed learner takes an active role in learning. In a conventional classroom setting this may be manifested in the learner seeking out every opportunity to understand, practise and learn (Carver and Dickinson 1982a: 15).

Thus the learner has the opportunity to negotiate the course (even minimally, simply by being aware of its objectives and monitoring their continued relevance) and so she becomes a participant in decision making rather than a passive object to whom things are done. Furthermore, teachers who seek opportunities to introduce a self-instructional mode, and who encourage the development of self-instruction, are demonstrating that they regard the learners as people with a positive attitude to learning who will accept and seek responsibility and are committed to achieving their objectives.

Emphasising the centrality of the learner may have several effects. Firstly, by giving enhanced importance to the learner, self-instruction may help to reduce the sense of inferiority and therefore lack of empathy for the language speakers often resulting from the learner's feelings of being a linguistic infant in the early stages of learning. Secondly, the learner's involvement in decision making may increase her motivation to achieve in language learning. There is evidence that when subordinates are able to exercise control (or participate in decision making) then productivity improves. Bachman (1964:272) argues that the increase in productivity results from an increase in an individual's motivation to perform effectively. Finally, there is evidence to support the common sense view that where learners are perceived by the teacher as committed to the achievement of learning objectives, as seeking and accepting responsibility, and as persons able to exercise control and self-direction, then they will behave in a way which confirms this perception. That is, they will live up to their reputations. By the same token, learners who are perceived negatively as disliking and avoiding study, who must be coerced, controlled and threatened with punishment, and who prefer to be directed, also confirm the perception by behaving in these ways (Bockman and Bockman 1972).

Affective factors

Many researchers and writers stress the importance of affective factors in language learning. (*Affective factors* are concerned with the learner's attitude towards the target language and users of it, and with her emotional responses. 'Affective' is often used in contrast to 'intellectual'.) Brown (1973), for example, discusses the importance of ethnocentric factors such as the learner's willingness or unwillingness to take on a new identity related to the target language; and social factors such as *empathy* 'the process of putting yourself into someone else's shoes – of reaching beyond the self, and understanding and feeling what another person is understanding and feeling'.

Schumann (1975) has investigated the importance of learner attitudes in success in language learning. He distinguishes:

- *Language shock*, which may produce feelings of dissatisfaction, frustration or guilt, at not being able to produce appropriate language or process it correctly;
- *Culture shock*, operative in target language culture, which may produce feelings of alienation or anxiety, coupled with defensive strategies such as rejection of native speaker values, and obsessional attachment to one's own values;
- *Language stress*, which he views in explicitly psychoanalytic terms, as a matter of affront to one's own narcissism because of a perceived deficiency in language, which commonly functions as a source of narcissistic gratification;
- *Anxiety*, consequent on the comic or infantile persona necessarily projected by the language learner.

A self-instructional learning mode can help to control these and other affective factors in the ways outlined below.

Empathy may be helped to develop within a group of learners by reducing the centrality of the teacher, so that her role becomes more that of a consultant. This is likely to increase the empathy between the teacher and learners, and this may have the effect of strengthening the bonding of a group of learners, reducing competition within the group, and increasing co-operation. Rogers (1969:118) argues that where the teacher is empathic, liking and affection are more evenly diffused around the group, and 'every student tends to feel liked by all the others – to have a more positive attitude towards himself and towards school.'

The major sources of *inhibition* for most language learners are the group of other learners within the class and, sometimes, the teacher. Inhibition increases as the feeling of competitiveness increases and decreases with the development of co-operation within the group. It is likely to be influenced by several factors related to the learning environment, some of which are discussed below under 'Extrinsic and Intrinsic Motivation'. Some forms of assessment are a major cause of inhibition; this can be reduced by increasing the amount of self-assessment. Similarly, an increase in individualisation and of self-access can work to reduce inhibition.

Assessment systems which value grades and scores over the actual learning that is achieved, reinforce attitudes of competition and so help to increase inhibition. There are few tests that assess increase in learning rather than simply count correct answers. Indeed it may be that any external evaluation, even that which is positive and praises the learner, has deleterious effects on the development of empathy and a co-operative atmosphere. Stevick (1980:23) warns against the 'evaluation paradigm' which consists of the teacher saying to the student 'Now try to do this so I can tell you how you did.' The student performs in some way, the teacher points out mistakes and the student's response to the task is evaluated. More importantly, 'the student generally comes away feeling that he himself has been evaluated negatively or positively – along with his product.'

I believe that self-assessment, individualisation and self-access will help to reduce inhibition and build confidence, and will help to increase empathy in the class. All three devices work to reduce competition, and at least one – self-access – may lead to an increase in co-operative learning.

In undertaking *self-assessment* learners reduce the need for the teacher to be involved in assessment and this helps to build greater empathy between teachers and learners. Furthermore there are opportunities in introducing self-assessment to emphasise learning rather than simply products – marks, grades and on. In addition, much self-assessment calls for two or more learners to work together, so encouraging co-operative learning. *Individualisation* reduces competition by making a better attempt than lockstep modes to match objectives and materials to individual learners' needs and level. Individualisation similarly reduces inhibition, partly because of the reduction of competition, but also because the tasks learners are asked to perform are likely to be more within their ability.

A self-instructional mode in which learners have *self-access* – direct access to resources – and in which they may be using these resources to work towards individual objectives, reduces competition, and therefore to an extent inhibition, in several ways. Firstly, and perhaps most importantly, it emphasises the multiplicity of resources – including people – available for learning. Thus a learner working in a self-access mode is likely to consult fellow students as well as the teacher about sources of information, appropriate materials and so on. Such co-operative learning can be actively fostered by the teacher by assigning group tasks. Secondly, as in individualisation, learners are likely to be involved in a variety of different tasks, so developing differing expertise. Further tasks can be designed, the solution of which will call on the newly acquired expertise of several learners, building co-operation and confidence simultaneously.

2.3.2 Wider educational goals

This section is concerned with two matters: the first is the development of general autonomy among members of society, and the second is concerned with ways of meeting the demands of society for the provision of continuing education.

Autonomy

Hitherto, we have been talking of autonomy as a mode of learning – one in which the individual is responsible for all of the decisions connected with her learning, and undertakes the implementation of these decisions. However, autonomy is being used here with a much wider meaning than autonomy in learning, though it includes that meaning.

The goals society has for education are ultimately much broader than simply the achievement of certain areas of knowledge and skills. In most societies the goals of the educational process will be in part concerned with sustaining that society in the current patterns, and with developing it in directions that are viewed as desirable. Thus education will be concerned with the development of people in ways broadly in sympathy with the current political milieu. A democratic society protects its democratic ideals through an educational process leading to independent individuals able to think for themselves. It is a principle of the educational systems of many such countries to foster autonomy.

What can we achieve as language teachers to further this important aim? Firstly, we must accept that language learning and teaching is a part of the total educational process, and therefore has to contribute to the achievement of wider educational aims. Secondly, we should recognise the potential of language learning and teaching as a facilitator of the development of autonomy – especially in the post-beginner stages. Assuming that autonomy grows through, *inter alia*, individuals being given practice in taking decisions and so accepting responsibility for their own learning, through co-operating with others in groups to work on problems and to produce a mutual solution, through exchanging ideas and opinions with others, and through discovering about authority figures and autonomous individuals through reading, then there are great opportunities for the development of autonomy in language teaching/learning.

The discussion above refers to autonomy as an educational objective to be achieved mainly at school level. For older people, learning opportunities may also help the growth of autonomy, but in addition the learning mode adopted is likely to be the more successful if it recognises and respects the adult as a self-directing individual. Thus I suggest that learning opportunities should offer the adult as much responsibility for her own learning as she can cope with; briefly, this might entail involving the learner in the analysis of her own needs, the specification of objectives, the selection of processes by which these objectives are to be met, and the assessment of how well they have been achieved.

Requirement for continuing education

There are economic, social and individual pressures on the educational system of a country to provide continuing education. The rate of change in modern society through technological developments, economic and commercial development and political groupings, may strain the ability of educational systems to cope. Mackenzie, Postgate and Scupham (1975:24) list several demands on educational systems to provide the skills required to cope with and exploit developments. They see demands for skills to operate and develop new activities created by technological advance, led today by developments in information technology and other computer developments. There are needs for skills to deal with the increasing internationalisation and mobility of economic and political life, for example multi-national, private and public undertakings, and new political groupings such as the European Common Market – all with evident implications for language learning. With the increase of knowledge and associated developments in technology, there are changes in equipment and processes which require a parallel development in specialist skills together with new patterns of work involving higher degrees of collaboration among specialists; this may also involve the use of different languages.

And last, but by no means least, there is the demand for opportunities for personal and cultural development, once again with implications for language learning. The strain on the agencies presently providing continuing education can be reduced by the adoption of some form of self-instructional mode. In addition the clients of continuing education frequently are just those who are unable to fit into the normal schedules of educational institutions and so a self-instructional mode may help to provide the learning opportunities required.

2.4 Motivation

The relationship between self-instruction and motivation is complex – as is motivation itself – and both deserve careful analysis. This section attempts to undertake such an analysis based on Gardner and Smythe's (1975:222) model of motivation, and extending it particularly with regard to learners' attitudes towards the learning situation. This extended model is discussed with reference to a self-instructional mode and the greater part of the discussion is concerned with questions about the learning situation. On the one hand some language teachers question whether it is possible for the learner to maintain her motivation to learn the language in a self-instructional mode, whilst on the other hand it is argued that many characteristics of self-instruction have a positive effect on instrinsic motivation. Finally, affective factors are important in motivation, and are closely interrelated with self-instruction, as has been demonstrated in section 2.3.1.

Gardner and Smythe's categorisation, together with Stern's (1983) commentary on it, has been used as a basis of the diagram in figure 4. This hypothesises an analysis of motivation extrapolating from Gardner and Smythe especially with regard to course related characteristics. It is important to note that in extrapolating away from Gardner and Smythe, we are also departing from hard evidence to a more speculative position drawing support from several sources.

2.4.1 Factors affecting motivation

The four main components of motivation shown on the diagram are based on Stern's (1983:384) discussion of Gardner's model. The components are:

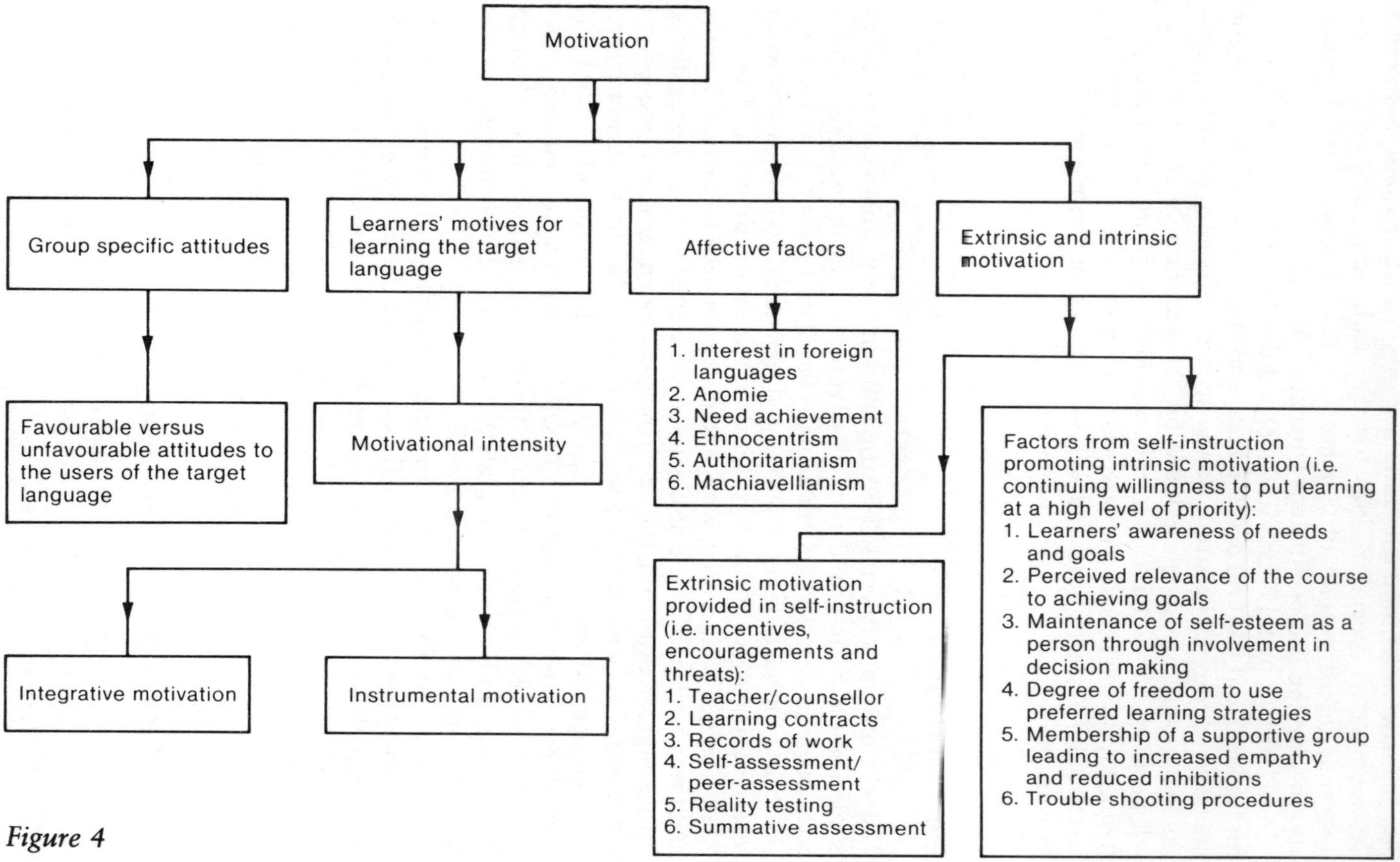

Motivation

Group specific attitudes

Learners' motives for learning the target language

Affective factors

Extrinsic and intrinsic motivation

Favourable versus unfavourable attitudes to the users of the target language

Motivational intensity

1. Interest in foreign languages
2. Anomie
3. Need achievement
4. Ethnocentrism
5. Authoritarianism
6. Machiavellianism

Factors from self-instruction promoting intrinsic motivation (i.e. continuing willingness to put learning at a high level of priority):

1. Learners' awareness of needs and goals
2. Perceived relevance of the course to achieving goals
3. Maintenance of self-esteem as a person through involvement in decision making
4. Degree of freedom to use preferred learning strategies
5. Membership of a supportive group leading to increased empathy and reduced inhibitions
6. Trouble shooting procedures

Extrinsic motivation provided in self-instruction (i.e. incentives, encouragements and threats):

1. Teacher/counsellor
2. Learning contracts
3. Records of work
4. Self-assessment/ peer-assessment
5. Reality testing
6. Summative assessment

Integrative motivation

Instrumental motivation

Figure 4

- Group-specific attitudes
- Learners' motives for learning the target language
- Affective factors (Stern's 'Generalized Attitudes') and
- Extrinsic and intrinsic motivation (Stern's 'Attitudes towards the learning situation')

The component of most interest to us is the final one – extrinsic and intrinsic motivation (see section 2.4.2). However, before discussing this I shall comment briefly on the others.

'Group-specific attitudes' refers to the attitudes of the learner toward the community of speakers of the target language. This category is unlikely to be affected directly by the mode of learning, but of course it is not static. Thus, as proficiency in the target language increases, so ethnocentrism is likely to decrease; and an increase in the learner's confidence may result in a growth of a more favourable attitude toward the language community. Finally, it is, of course, an important responsibility of both teachers and materials to promote a favourable attitude to the target language.

'Learners' motives for learning the target language' divide into the well-known distinction between integrative and instrumental. Integrative motivation, which is the desire to be accepted by the community of speakers of the target language, has close links with the category 'group-specific attitudes'. Instrumental motivation derives from the need to learn the target language for job or education-related purposes. The two are not in opposition and any particular learner may have both kinds of motivation in some degree. Moreover, the intensity of these different motivational causes can change as the learner's experience develops. A visit to the country or area in which the target language is spoken might result in a boost for integrative motivation (Gardner and Smythe 1975:228).

Regarding 'affective factors', Gardner and Smythe found that *interest in foreign languages* correlated with success in language learning as did *anomie*, which refers to feelings of dissatisfaction with one's role in society, and *need achievement*, which is a measure of one's need to succeed in everything one does. Three variables are negatively related to achievement in French: *ethnocentrism*, the viewing of one's own language group as superior; *authoritarianism* which is ethnocentric, uncritical of authority figures, conforming, traditionalist and prejudice prone; and *machiavellianism*, which is an index of an individual's tendency to want to manipulate others.

2.4.2. Extrinsic and intrinsic motivation

Some teachers question whether learners would have the necessary 'motivation' to learn in a self-instructional mode; that is, they question whether learners would continue to learn without extrinsic motivation – the incentives, encouragement and threats provided by both the teacher and the educational context.

First, I must stress that self-instruction does not entail a withdrawal from the student of help in structuring her learning. There are many varieties and degrees of self-instruction (see Chapter 1) and it is only when the learner becomes autonomous that she undertakes the whole management of her own learning. So far as incentives, encouragement and threats are concerned, these may still be provided by the teacher, but other agencies, including the learner and her peers, are also recruited to help. In addition devices like the learning contract described in Chapter 6 provide an incentive to the learner to complete her allotted portion of work. Self-assessment techniques, which are described in detail in Appendix D(I), are important in assessing when objectives have been achieved, and in general, in charting progress through a course of study without creating an unduly evaluative atmosphere. Finally, summative assessment is not the exclusive preserve of conventional learning modes, and is available in self-instruction also.

Self-instruction is, of course, concerned with helping learners to develop their own, intrinsic, motivation. I define this to mean the learner's continued willingness to put learning the target language at a high level of priority among all the demands on her time. The relationship between self-instruction and intrinsic motivation is presented in the diagram, and each factor is discussed below.

Within a self-instructional learning mode there is a higher degree of likelihood that the learner will be aware of her needs and goals. This may be because she has special needs for the target language, or it may be because the teacher has discussed needs and goals with the learners as part of the process of facilitating self-direction. Following the learner's awareness of her needs and goals is her perception of the relevance of the course of study in helping her to achieve those goals; and an important factor within this is the learner's power to change or adjust the course if it is not relevant to the goals.

The learner's involvement in decision making also has a positive effect on motivation. Firstly there is evidence (Bachman 1964) that involvement in decision making tends to result in increased productivity through increased motivation to perform effectively. Secondly such involvement may have the effect of building, or at least maintaining, the learner's self-esteem. A course which makes you feel good – and important – is more likely to be motivating than one which makes you feel small and foolish.

The degree of freedom the learner has to use preferred learning techniques is also likely to have an effect on motivation. Carver (1984) while recognising that some learning techniques are likely to be more productive than others, argues that 'any (technique) sincerely adopted by a learner as a way of coping is more likely to help than not', on the grounds that the personal assumption by the learner of responsibility for her own learning is a fundamental prerequisite for success in language learning. By contrast, if the learner is prevented from using her favoured techniques this is likely to seem to her to reduce her learning effectiveness and so be de-motivating. Thus, a learner who checks her understanding of the target language by asking for confirmation of her own interpretation, or by asking for simplification, and who is regularly denied this by the teacher, for whatever reason and no matter how kindly, is likely to be de-motivated.

However, this is not a simple matter. One of the teacher's responsibilities is to help learners develop the most effective learning techniques, and this may involve getting some learners to change from ineffective techniques. Many teachers achieve this through negotiation, always treating the learner as responsible but presenting themselves in the valid role of experts in learning techniques.

I have argued above that self-instruction, involving as it does a change in the role of the teacher, leads to increased empathy between teacher and learners and among learners. This, together with the emphasis on co-operative learning in self-instruction, leads to a more cohesive and supportive group of learners which is motivating in several ways, but in particular is likely to lead to a reduction of inhibition.

A feature of the preparation for self-directed learning proposed by Dickinson and Carver (1981, 1982a) is 'trouble shooting' – a regular classroom session in which students are encouraged to specify just what they find difficult in their learning. This is likely to be a positive motivating factor in general since it demonstrates concern on the part of the teacher for the individual learner's problems, so increasing her sense of self-worth; and in particular it is likely to be motivating in that it helps to remove barriers to the smooth progression of learning.

2.5 Learning how to learn foreign languages

Cutting across many of the previous justifications for self-instruction in learning foreign languages is the need to help people to learn how to learn, both to realise many of the aims embodied in these justifications, and as an important educational aim in its own right. Thus, meeting the needs for continuing education, and particularly, facilitating language learning for those who for practical reasons cannot take conventional courses, and finally, helping individuals to achieve autonomy, all entail assisting potential learners to learn how to learn. But more radical than this, many teachers and educationalists see learning how to learn as the most basic and important educational objective, no matter what teaching/learning mode is adopted. Rogers (1969:104) states the need boldly: 'The only man who is educated is the man who has learned how to learn; the man who has learned how to adapt and change; the man who has realized that no knowledge is secure, that only the process of *seeking* knowledge gives a basis for security.'

Learning how to learn is in a sense what much of this book is about. It is a matter first of developing knowledge about learning processes – and about oneself as a learner, secondly of planning learning, and thirdly of discovering and then using appropriate and preferred strategies to achieve the objectives specified by the plans. Flavell (1979:906) uses the term 'metacognition' to describe this ability, and analyses it into the following elements:

- *Metacognitive knowledge*: what you know about learning and yourself with respect to learning (for example, 'I find it difficult to remember grammar rules').
- *Metacognitive experiences*: conscious cognitive or affective experiences that accompany any intellectual exercise, (for example, realising that one does or does not understand something).
- *Goals or tasks*: the objectives of a cognitive activity or enterprise.
- *Action or strategies*: how an individual goes about achieving her objectives (for example, monitoring progress; or deciding always to make an informed guess about the meaning of a word before looking it up in the dictionary). (See also Chapter 7 section 4.)

Learning about a new subject, such as beginning to learn a foreign language, may be largely a matter of developing metacognitive knowledge about it. Thus the learner has to discover what are appropriate learning strategies for her, through trying out the kinds of activities the teacher advises, and through trying out strategies from other learning experiences. The results will be stored as metacognitive knowledge and the activity of trying them out will be metacognitive experiences. Stern's characterisation of the good language learner summarised above can be seen in terms of the individual's successful development of metacognition – or learning to learn – with respect to modern languages.

Finally, learning how to learn a foreign language is a desirable prerequisite of some learner-centred methods. This is particularly true of those which are concerned with giving learners opportunities to practise using the language for communicative purposes; many teachers using such methods are, consciously or not, involved in helping their students to learn how to learn. The most effective way to give learners opportunities to use the target language communicatively is to divide the class into pairs or small groups. In doing this, the teacher is freeing the learners from detailed control over what they say and how they say it, and since the teacher can attend to only one group at a time, the learners themselves must take on many responsibilities for their own learning.

2.6 Conclusion

The question 'why adopt self-instruction?' was answered by arguing that a self-instructional mode was useful in solving practical problems of learners, and in helping to achieve several educational aims. Prominent among these was the development of personal autonomy and the improvement of learning efficiency. The chapter also indicated a connection between self-instruction and motivation. The following chapters, concerned as they are with the practical implementation of self-instruction, set out to demonstrate how these claims can be justified.

Part II
Facilitating learning: introduction

Self-instruction clearly entails that the learners themselves undertake more of the tasks associated with learning without the assistance of a teacher. There are various degrees of this learning mode, the ultimate being autonomy, in which the learner is responsible for all of the decisions concerned with her learning, and carries out all of the necessary activities. In order to identify the tasks the learner must undertake at the various levels of self-instruction – and subsequently to look for ways in which the learner can be helped in undertaking these tasks – we must first attempt to discover what the teacher does in a conventional teaching/ learning context to facilitate learning. The table in figure 5 (based on Allwright 1978 and Hilsum and Strong 1978) attempts to record the major tasks of the teacher.

The extent to which learners take over these tasks in a self-instructional mode depends on the degree of independence they wish to undertake; it is the purpose of this book to investigate what is *possible* for learners, and to suggest how learners can be prepared for and helped to undertake those responsibilities and activities. To argue that something is possible is by no means the same as arguing that it is desirable, and the degree of independence desirable for any particular learner depends on matters like age, previous experience of language learning, level, and perhaps most important of all, inclination. The view expressed here is that learners should have as much responsibility for their learning as they can cope with at the particular age and level they are at; and that teachers, having passed on to the learners those responsibilities and consequent tasks which they can cope with, should use their resulting freedom firstly to promote greater independence among learners by preparing them for greater self-direction, and secondly to concentrate on those tasks which the learners find hardest to undertake for themselves. Instances include monitoring and correcting spoken utterances, providing encouragement and motivation, and assisting with activities such as needs analysis and the identification of appropriate materials.

However, in the application of this view, we must take into account the various instructional contexts in which learners may be operating. At one end of the scale there is the modern language class at school level with all the external pressures of rigid timetabling, centralised curriculum and the need to work for an external examination. At the other end of the scale there is the language learning provision made in a university for individuals who have particular language learning needs. Here there are fewer restrictions exerted by timetabling and there may be no requirements on the learners to take examinations. The possibilities of introducing self-instruction in the first context are greatly restricted and techniques have to be found which are suitable to the context. Chapter 3 is devoted to examining self-instructional schemes both at school level and for adults, and Chapter 7 offers some suggestions of how self-instruction might be introduced in the school classroom.

The table in figure 5 shows in the left-hand column the major tasks undertaken by the language teacher, and in the right-hand column there are suggestions of how these can be fulfilled in a self-instructional learning mode. The following chapters in Part II are concerned with describing ways in which each of these tasks can be undertaken in self-instruction, so that each entry in the right-hand column is discussed in detail in a later chapter.

The first group of tasks for which the teacher is responsible is that under the heading of 'Pedagogical planning' which includes both 'Needs analysis' and 'Selection of materials'. Needs analysis in a conventional classroom approach to language teaching is a matter for the teacher (or more probably an educational administrator at school level), deciding on the long-term aims of language learning for all of the students in a course, or even in the country. A self-instructional mode can cope with different needs for each individual; and the needs themselves, and the objectives to meet those needs can be specified through a needs analysis questionnaire used either by the learner alone, or by the learner in consultation with a tutor. The design of needs analysis questionnaires, and their application, is discussed in the first part of Chapter 5.

The selection of materials to meet the learners' needs is once again done centrally within a conventional classroom-based system, whilst in a self-instructional mode the materials may either be selected by the learner (with help from a tutor) from a self-access resource, or the learner is offered some kind of package of materials which are appropriate to his needs. The two different systems are described in Chapter 3, and ways of organising self-access materials are described in Chapter 6. In both cases, however, there is a need to select and/or design materials which are suitable for self-instruction. In some systems the learner is encouraged to become involved in the design of his own learning materials, based on authentic texts. This is particularly true in the system used in CRAPEL at the University of Nancy II in France. However, in most systems, the materials are selected or designed by a tutor. Guidelines for the selection and design of self-instructional materials are offered in Chapter 4.

The second major group of tasks for which the teacher is responsible (in the left-hand column of the table) is headed 'Teaching' and includes both

The major tasks of the teacher	*Alternative agencies in self-instruction*
1 Pedagogical planning	
1.1 *Needs analysis*	
– Determining long-term aims	Needs analysis questionnaire
– Determining short-term objectives	
1.2 *Selection of materials*	
– Selecting course books/materials to meet objectives	Packaging – for example, Circle Model
– Selecting supplementary materials	Self-access
– Selecting materials suitable for self-instruction	No alternative
2 Teaching	
2.1 *Preparatory*	
– Selecting lesson topic/teaching items	Learner contract
– Planning lesson	
– Devising tasks	
2.2 *Actual teaching*	
– Determining occurrence of the target language	Course materials and/or contract
– Determining other content	
– Determining task type	
– Determining aspiration level of performance	
– Determining time distribution	
– Presentation of new material	Course materials/native speaker informants
– Providing explanations and descriptions	
– Teacher answers questions	
– Teacher monitors responses	

– Teacher leads discussion – Teacher asks questions/selects respondents	Peer group or 'study buddy'
– Teacher counsels (circulates round room)	Best done by teacher/helper Peers may help
3 Assessment	
3.1 *Preparatory*	
– Selection/design of tests and exercises	For some assessment purposes can be done by learner and peers
3.2 *Actual*	
– Conducts test	For some purposes can be conducted by learner or peer
– Allocates homework – Sets exercises etc.	Contract; learner
3.3 *Post-lesson*	
– Marks/grades the test or exercise with/without learners	For some purposes can be self-graded or peer-graded
– Discusses result with learner	No satisfactory alternative
– Takes remedial action	Could be built into materials
4 Management and organisational activities	
4.1 *Materials and equipment*	
– Gives out, takes in books and equipment	Self-access, through resource centre
– Arranges, checks equipment	Librarian/teacher in charge and/or learner

The major tasks of the teacher	*Alternative agencies in self-instruction*
4.2 *Organises learners*	
– Determines who does what with whom – for example, arranges pairs, groups etc.	Arranged by learners
– Determines and implements general standards of behaviour	In some contexts teacher's authority required, but peer group might assist
4.3 *Record keeping*	
– Keeps register of attendance	Probably still necessary
– Keeps records of grades etc.	Still necessary but also kept by learner
– Record of work completed	(Still necessary but also kept by learner)
5 Counselling and Supporting	
5.1 *Motivating*	Even more important in self-instruction
5.2 *Supporting*	
– Congratulating	
– Commiserating	
5.3 *Counselling*	
– Discusses learning problems	
– Gives advice about materials	
– Gives general advice	
5.4 *Interacting*	
– General interaction to establish rapport	

Figure 5

preparation for teaching and the actual teaching itself. Many of the decisions which have to be made under 'Preparatory' can be made by the learner in a self-instructional mode with the help of the needs questionnaire mentioned above and with the 'Learner contract' described in Chapter 5.

Many of the decisions and tasks listed under the label 'Actual teaching' (2.2) can be carried out by four agencies other than the teacher: the materials being used; native, or competent speakers of the target language; peers; and the learner himself. This area is treated in a number of places: in Chapter 3, which describes various systems of self-instruction; in Chapter 4, which is concerned with materials, and in Chapter 5, which looks at ways of supporting the learner. The third major area of responsibility for the teacher is 'Assessment', which is dealt with in Chapter 8.

The teacher in a conventional system is also responsible for a whole range of management and organisational activities, listed under section 4 in the left-hand column of the table. Thus, teachers are responsible for giving out and taking in books and equipment and so on. Within a self-access, self-instructional system the learners themselves are responsible for the selection of the appropriate materials from the self-access resources. Suggestions about how these might be organised and run are made in Chapter 6. The organisation of groups etc., and maintaining appropriate standards of behaviour is normally the responsibility of the teacher. There appears to be no good reason why learners cannot take over these functions, and indeed many teachers pass to learners the responsibility for organising themselves into groups. On the occasions when it is desirable to pair or group learners in particular ways – one strong with one weak learner for example – the teacher can intervene with suggestions.

The third area of management and organisation under section 4 is in the table 'Record keeping'. The record keeping of grades is treated in Chapter 8. The other records of work can easily be kept by learners (where necessary the teacher can keep her own records in addition). The keeping of records is discussed in Chapters 3 and 5. Finally, the teacher in a conventional mode is responsible for counselling and supporting the learners. These tasks are probably best carried out by a teacher whatever mode (short of autonomy) is used, although peers and peer support groups can assist. This is discussed in Chapter 5.

Part II, then, is concerned with the implementation of self-instructional systems; the materials the learners need, how learners might be helped and supported in this learning mode, how the physical resources might be organised, and ways in which both learners and teachers can be prepared for self-instruction. In order to place these considerations in a meaningful context, Part II begins with a chapter describing seven different systems of self-instruction, four at adult level, and three at school level. Chapter 4 then examines in detail the specialised needs for learning materials this learning mode has, and Chapter 5 suggests some of the ways learners can be supported whilst using a self-instructional mode. One way of helping to support learners, and of making learning materials available, is through a self-access resource centre. Chapter 6 identifies important factors in setting up and running such a centre. Chapter 7 addresses the most important of all these matters – the preparation of both learners and teachers for self-instruction.

3 Self-instructional systems

Though there is no doubt that learning materials are central to self-instruction, it is not possible to give any straightforward description of such materials. This is because the requirements on learning materials differ considerably according to the approach that is taken to self-instruction. Different approaches differ according to several variables. One set of variables relates to the needs the system sets out to meet. These include the number of foreign languages being offered – one or many; attempts to meet varying specific needs within a language; attempts to provide learning possibilities at one or many levels. A second set of variables relates to the attitudes of the organisers towards what they see as appropriate self-instructional materials. Thus it may be felt that only specially prepared materials are appropriate; or it may be felt that only authentic texts should be used, and that learners should learn to use them for instructional purposes; or the attitude may favour eclecticism, so that published materials, specially prepared materials and authentic texts are all used. The third and final set of variables concerns the constraints imposed by the parent institution in which the self-instructional system is operating. Thus a comprehensive school for example may have major timetable and accommodation constraints compared say to a private language school or a language learning facility within a university.

Rather than attempt to discuss learning materials immediately, I will begin by describing some self-instructional systems which illustrate these variables, and then examine in more detail the requirements these systems have for materials. We can then go on from this to examine ways of supporting learners in self-instructional systems, and finally draw together the requirements for setting up self-access resource centres. The first four systems described provide facilities for adult learners. We will then examine more briefly three systems used in secondary schools.

3.1 Systems used for adult learners

The systems selected for description are first that run by the Centre de Recherches et d'Applications Pédagogiques en Langues (CRAPEL) in the

University of Nancy II, France; the second is the Open Access Sound and Video Library at the University of Cambridge, the third is a system designed by James McCafferty for the British Council, and the fourth is that used in the Scottish Centre for Education Overseas at Moray House.

3.1.1 CRAPEL

CRAPEL provide facilities for self-directed learning of English for learners within the university, learners who are extramural, and 'on-site' groups, i.e. groups of employees in local factories and commercial organisations. Learners have the choice between following a 'normal' evening class course or learning autonomously. Those who choose the latter do so either because of practical considerations like inability to attend the course or specialist requirements in English which the course would not cater for, or from choice because they have had good reports of self-directed learning from friends and colleagues. For CRAPEL however, the provision of a self-directed learning facility is central to their philosophy. Besides a commitment to self-instruction to cater for those for whom 'normal' evening class provision is inappropriate, they have a powerful ideological commitment to autonomy in learning. This commitment is based on the inherent desirability of autonomy for the adult, and the recognition of the serious limitation of classroom teaching, and course and textbooks: '... the adult who undertakes language instruction does so for relatively precise reasons, usually professional ones (with the result that most individuals have their own set of objectives) which conflicts with the most basic assumption of traditional classroom teaching, namely, that all present need to learn the same thing.' (Riley 1974:4) And in general: 'Autonomy is an experiment in how learning can be freed from the bonds of any institution, and in how the individual can reclaim control of and responsibility for his or her own education, while investigating the opportunities to learn from a variety of authentic sources.' (Stanchina 1975)

Learners enrolling for English classes at CRAPEL have the choice between immediately undertaking an autonomous programme and enrolling for a 'normal' evening class course which simultaneously prepares them for autonomy. On-site courses vary enormously in content and organisation, but usually include preparation for autonomous work.

Learners who opt for autonomy are allocated to a 'helper' – a native or competent speaker of English experienced in assisting autonomous learners – and together they work towards establishing the learner's needs and goals, identifying constraints such as time available for learning and ability to come to CRAPEL, and finally they make preliminary decisions about materials, methods and techniques of learning.

Most learners opting to work autonomously are non-beginners, but if the learner is a beginner the helper is able to offer modules of material dealing with particular functions in English. (These 'modules' are used with non-beginners too, on the principle of the cyclical syllabus.) Non-beginners may be asked to take a placement test, and on the basis of this, materials will (initially at least) be prepared by the helper, based on texts of relevant content. As the learning progresses the learners take on a greater and greater share of the responsibility for all aspects of their learning, including the selection of materials and even the design of activities. Total autonomy from the institution is the ultimate aim, but in the meantime the helper is available to assist with all aspects of learning.

The role of the helper in the CRAPEL system is concerned chiefly with helping the learner to learn how to learn. This includes analysing needs, learning about techniques for using authentic texts, learning how to find materials and how to use them, and helping with matters such as organisation of time and so on. The helper resists becoming a language teacher, and tries to prevent helping sessions from becoming merely private tutorials. The learner's pedagogical situation is that of semi-autonomy, and one of the purposes of the prepared materials the learner is using is to show him techniques which he can use on other materials. In addition, CRAPEL offer taught group sessions devoted to providing descriptive knowledge of such linguistic concepts as register, grammar and lexis, and practical demonstrations of different kinds of exercises.

Besides having large resources of printed authentic materials, and learning materials prepared by CRAPEL staff, learners also have access to the Sound and Video Library. This houses a wide selection of authentic sound and video recordings, catalogued according to subject and level of difficulty, and a selection of hardware which can be used for playing them. However, sound recordings are usually just copied onto the learner's own cassette and taken away for work at home.

Assessment in the CRAPEL system is carried out by the learner himself, and rather than using independent tests only remotely connected with the materials, is fully contextualised, making estimates of things like performance on the materials, comprehension of native speakers, degree of understanding/misunderstanding by native speakers of the learner's performance and so on. Since the materials used are selected to be as relevant as possible to the objectives of the learner, this contextualising of assessment makes a great deal of sense.

Another aspect of CRAPEL's work in developing language learning is concerned with 'on-site' courses for local organisations. CRAPEL handles between four and ten such contracts annually for hospitals, offices, factories, research centres and so on. Before undertaking a contract, a member of staff from CRAPEL assesses the requirement and, where he considers it appropriate, recommends some level of self-directed work. In these cases the tutor's task is mainly to prepare the students for autonomy, as described above.

An example of such a scheme was that set up for retired people at the *Université de Troisième Age*. The original request for English classes was expressed in very vague terms, and there were several serious logistical problems; for example, no rooms were available, and there was not enough money to pay for a traditional teacher-staffed course. CRAPEL suggested a modified autonomous course since a typical autonomous course would not have been suitable. An important requirement of the group was the social contact, and this was as important as the learning of English. Consequently, a scheme of autonomous groups was developed. The learners, with advice from CRAPEL, divided themselves into groups (mainly on the basis of friendship grouping, though true beginners formed a separate group). At the beginning, four afternoons were spent preparing the students for autonomous learning. From there on, the groups developed their own work schedules, which tended to be two sessions per week of about two hours each. The groups were assigned helpers, who advised on techniques and materials, and all the participants had access to the Sound and Video Library. The helpers also provided assistance on such matters as how to tackle a particular problem, made suggestions on what activities to do, provided materials – recordings, courses, songs and so on – and contacted native speakers and got them to come along regularly to group meetings. After some initial doubts, the learners developed a great liking for autonomy; they appreciated the freedom of choice and action, which was not available in an institution. The scheme ran for five years, but is now in abeyance. A similar scheme for university technical and administrative staff is now under way.

3.1.2 The Cambridge system

Note: The Cambridge system is currently undergoing modification in several important areas, so that at the time of writing the system described is partially as it is operating, partially experimental and partially as planned.

The Open Access Sound and Video Library in the University of Cambridge, begun in 1966, aims at offering language learning facilities to the members of the University. The users include undergraduates, postgraduates and staff members all with a great diversity of needs. Some need to learn a foreign language well enough to cope whilst in the foreign country for a conference, or as a tourist; others require a very high degree of proficiency in a rare language spoken in a country where they wish to carry out field work. The majority of the users are non-specialist language learners and are from a wide selection of the faculties of the University. Their motivation varies widely, the time available to them for learning a foreign language varies enormously, and there are no examinations to sustain failing enthusiasm. The system aims to offer individuals the opportunity of learning a language of their choice – at present the system offers over one hundred languages – beginning at any point during the year, at times which are convenient to them and at their own pace. The system takes advantage of the University's traditional preference for independent study (Harding-Esch 1982: 14).

The Cambridge Open Access Library is founded on the idea that a language learning system should be learner-centred and motivation-based, and that learners should be encouraged to become autonomous. The urge towards autonomy is based on the organisers' view of the nature of the language learning process and on the view that autonomy is an educational objective appropriate to this society. However, the encouragement towards autonomy implies that the majority of learners start from a point of dependence and so need help to become autonomous; and that some learners either choose to remain dependent or are unable to achieve autonomy. For these it is counter-productive to thrust autonomy on them and so other arrangements must be made. For this reason the self-access resource centre has been complemented with an advisory service. This service is independent of the self-access centre, and located in a different place. When University members contact the advisory service before using the self-access facility, the adviser may in fact recommend some not to use the self-access facility because he judges it to be an inappropriate learning mode for that person. Taught language courses are offered in addition to the self-access mode, so that in principle anyway, the self-access facilities cannot be perceived as a 'second best' solution, but as a positive choice. (At present only French and German at post 'O' level and post 'A' level are offered.)

The self-access system is presently based in a language laboratory of conventional format with thirty-two audio-active-comparative booths and three booths equipped with video playback. The catalogue of materials is on open access in the foyer of the laboratory. There are plans to re-design the system in such a way that space is distributed according to the learning activities available (a listening corner, a viewing corner (pre-recorded videos or live reception by satellite), a CAL corner, a reading area, etc.)

The main functions of the advisory service are:

- to provide information to students about the existence and resources of the self-access system;

– to provide information about materials, help learners to choose materials and prepare new materials;
– to provide information about the assessment procedures available and to help learners to assess their own progress;
– to help and advise learners about such things as needs identification, short-term objectives, what is feasible in the time available and possible learning strategies;
– to provide help to learners in such things as finding other learners of a particular language, finding native speakers willing to act as informants, forming groups and so on;
– to provide information on taught courses which exist when the adviser judges it appropriate for the client, and in certain special cases, organise supervision.

Through this advisory service many of the requirements arising from the organisers' pedagogical philosophy are met. Thus the adviser is able to guide and help learners towards autonomy and is prepared to give additional help to those who find autonomy difficult to achieve.

The self-access system offers a wide range of materials; it caters for over one hundred languages and some kind of language laboratory course is available for each of these. In addition, for the more commonly taught languages there is a wide range of different types of course allowing for different levels, objectives and styles of learning. There is also a range of 'modules' or chunks of material tackling a range of, or particular, teaching points. And for many languages there are audio and video recordings. Software for computer-assisted language learning is being planned. Naturally, not all the courses are suitable for self-instruction and in some cases the learner is, in the first instance, given the Teacher's Book, which is a less than satisfactory solution. The organiser's task includes adapting such courses whenever possible so that they are more suitable for self-instruction.

How does the system actually work? Let us suppose that a postgraduate student wishes to learn Arabic in order to go to Jordan to do field work. He might be told about the self-access facilities by his supervisor, and when he went to the Sound and Video Library he would discover on the outside door a chart showing the layout. In the foyer to the language laboratory he would find a copy of the 'Square One Kit'. This is a self-explanatory folder containing all the information necessary for using the library. It contains leaflets giving advice and information on the catalogue, and on how to analyse language learning needs. It also contains demonstration cassettes on how to use the machines in the laboratory and how to make use of authentic documents. The learner can look through the catalogue, discover a course in Arabic and get on with it.

For non-specialist language learners, however, one of a number of alternative courses of action may be more advisable. Firstly, he would be advised in a leaflet in the Square One Kit to think carefully about why he wishes to learn Arabic, what use he will make of it and so on. This leaflet suggests a number of questions he can profitably ask himself under the headings of *Motivation*, *Aims*, *Functions*, *Information*, and *Activities* (Harding-Esch, 1982: 16, and see also 5.1.1). Secondly the learner may immediately, or after some time, seek help from the adviser. The help he seeks may be concerned with problems of the materials available. In this case the adviser may be able to suggest additional or alternative materials, or may be able to link him with a native speaker of the language. Or the learner may be having difficulty with learning in an autonomous mode. In this case the adviser can offer advice and help with autonomous learning and perhaps suggest strategies that the learner could adopt to help overcome his particular problems. Or he may judge that such a learning mode is inappropriate for this student at this time and recommend that he follows one of the taught courses that this service also supplies.

A learner planning to learn or extend his knowledge of a language may go directly to the adviser without first visiting the Sound and Video Library. In this case the adviser might recommend a self-access approach, possibly because he feels it is appropriate to this learner, or possibly because there is no alternative for the particular language (or level) the learner wishes to learn. Where it is appropriate and feasible the adviser may recommend that the learner joins one of the intensive language classes run by the service. Finally, a learner may enrol for one of these classes directly and supplement his learning through the self-access facilities, perhaps with the help of the adviser, and/or continue his language learning using a self-access mode.

3.1.3 The British Council

James McCafferty's proposals, developed in 1981–82, derive from an analysis made of self-access systems and the possibility of using such systems in the Direct Teaching of English Operation (DTEO) of the British Council as an alternative to conventional teacher-led instruction (McCafferty 1982, McCafferty ND). Consequently the system he describes is one offering a total package, rather than being annexed to conventional class instruction. For McCafferty:

> The essence of 'self-access' is that the learner is in control of his or her own learning whenever he or she wants to be but only then. ... if the 'prescribed syllabus' approach tends to force learners along a single, narrow and often unsuitable road to where they do not particularly want to go, then 'total

autonomy' may be akin to abandoning the learner, without map or compass, in the middle of a very foreign field. 'Self-access' is the local, friendly travel agent. (ND: 1)

McCafferty sets out to design a self-access system which would cater for adult learners with specific needs for English whose entry levels vary from beginner to relatively advanced. Since it was proposed for the British Council's DTEO it had to be self-financing, and consequently satisfy consumers that they were receiving value for money.

His solution is, to continue his own analogy, one of supplying maps of increasing scale to the learners to enable them first to discover where they are, and then where they wish to get to – the 'Performance Chart'; and then to supply large scale maps of the successive steps towards the destination – 'Networks'. The learners are given whatever assistance they need by a team of 'helpers' – specialists in language learning and teaching whose role is to provide help to the learner and to develop the system by finding and writing materials, developing assessment instruments, indexes and so on.

The easiest way to describe McCafferty's system is to follow an imaginary learner through it from entry to exit. Unfortunately not only is the learner imaginary but the system itself exists only in McCafferty's papers. It has not been possible (at the time of writing) for the British Council to initiate a trial scheme; nor, sadly, are his papers easily obtainable.

The example system described by McCafferty is designed for civil service administrators in a European country. The learner entering the system would first consult a helper who would work with him to establish his aspiration level in various skill areas, priorities within these skill areas, and starting level. The key document to define starting level, aspiration level, and the stages along the way is the Performance Chart. (See figure 6.)

This has nine levels – from beginner to virtual native speaker competence – and nine skill areas relevant to administrators. The nine skill areas consist of three aspects of the general reading skill, three aspects of the writing skill and three of the oral skills of listening and speaking. Each of the 81 resulting boxes contains a description of the criterial behaviour for that skill at that level. For example, the skill area 'Listen/Speak – Give, exchange information, check, report repair' at level 4 requires that the learner 'can make appointments, check, cancel, alter' and importantly, that he can also undertake all the tasks described at levels 3 through to 0 for that skill. A learner wishing to achieve level 7 for this skill would first work on level 5, then on 6 and finally on level 7. And this, of course, is true for the other skills. The Performance Chart, then, provides a very simple way of identifying needs, relating needs to goals and identifying intermediate goals. It also gives guidance about the learner's entry competence, though the helper may suggest that the learner uses a simple proficiency test to confirm the entry level.

Once entry and aspiration levels have been identified, the learner will wish to find materials to help him to work towards the next level. This is where the Network comes in. Each box of the performance chart has a Network associated with it. A Network is essentially a set of related modules of language materials associated with a set of written, spoken and/or video texts. The behavioural goals described in each block of the Performance Chart have been broken down into objectives and the associated Network will enable the learner to achieve the objectives and, consequently, the goal. The imaginary learner, then, would be guided to the appropriate Network for his first step. A Network is illustrated in figure 7, which is adapted from McCafferty (ND: 15).

The focal point of a Network is a block of associated texts (a text may be written, spoken or video), with one text being central. The texts are short in the lower levels and get progressively longer at the higher levels. However the texts even at level 9 are only about 500 words, which is one page of printed text. Besides the central text, each Network would require something like 10 texts on the same topic as the central text, 20 texts at about the same level, 15 more advanced texts, 15 simpler texts and 5 video sequences. All of the written texts would also be recorded on cassette giving 60 audio texts. For each text there is a support sheet which supplies meaning through illustrations and translation of key words and phrases. The key document in a Network is the Pathways Sheet. This is an index of all the learning materials in the Network. Thus, referring to the illustrated Network in figure 7, each of the boxes would have an entry on the Pathways Sheet. From this the learner can see at a glance what the materials cover. The texts are indexed separately with information on Level, Skill, Topic and Medium. In addition each text is numbered, and the higher numbers indicate that more work is required for that text.

Neither the Performance Chart nor the Networks are intended to be restrictive. They are guides to the learner of where he is, where he wishes to go and how to get there. Thus, though our imaginary learner would see that box 4 would be the first step towards his goal, there is nothing to prevent him working on box 5 for example, or from working on two boxes at once. The helper would be available to give advice and may suggest that working on a single level or maybe two would limit the learner's objectives and give him a better idea of achievement, but the decision is the learner's. Similarly there is no 'right way' through a Network.

TARGET SKILL	LISTEN/SPEAK	LISTEN/SPEAK	LISTEN/SPEAK	WRITE
SCALE	*Give, exchange information, check, report, repair.*	*Give, exchange, ask for views, comment, discuss, clarify.*	*Socialise, react, repair, vary register, convey attitude.*	*Enquire, sound out, ask for information, initiate correspondence.*
9	Presents clearly and follows all that is said in group discussion.	Can negotiate at all levels, responds effectively, persuasively.	Can deal effectively with total strangers even on the telephone, control and initiate.	Can gather information from any source or make almost any initial contact.
8	Can report clearly on events, meetings and follow what is reported individually.	Can offer appreciation, alternatives, evaluate possibilities and means.	Can recognise and respond to irony, jokes, misunderstandings.	Has wide range of styles and registers and has a clear, logical approach.
7	Recognises different styles of interaction and implication and colloquial language.	Can discuss a detailed plan or proposal with those with shared knowledge.	Can function in group of strangers, discuss topics outside work.	Can choose appropriate form of language to suit a range of correspondents.
6	Can get and give information face to face with native speakers.	Could interview or be interviewed by non-hostile native speaker.	Could act as guide/ official, host to visitors, colleagues.	Can sustain logical chain of questions, direct or implied, in familiar topic areas.
5	Can report and understand simple events and actions in the past.	Can express approval, doubt, hesitation, but misses finer points of degree.	Can present himself, make introductions, invitations, accept, refuse over meals.	Can make standard enquiries of a routine, impersonal nature.
4	Can make appointments, arrangements, check, cancel, alter.	Can discuss aspects of own work and immediate work environment.	Can express personal likes, dislikes, preferences, opinions.	Can produce individual 'stock' questions, one at a time.
3	Can describe job, give and follow routine instructions.	Can state own position in very broad terms, but not able to justify.	Can function in shops, hotels, travelling, and exchange personal details.	Can produce simple yes/no or 'WH' question forms.
2	Can give personal information, recognise predictable questions.	Is limited to 'good', 'bad' and 'don't know' or 'don't care'.	Can survive on a set of 'stock phrases' in defined situations.	Can produce a very few memorised questions about time, person, place.
1	Knows a number of words and phrases but is limited by poor production and recognition			Can produce the odd question when most of the information is supplied by the situation.
0	Can exchange the odd word or phrase but no meaningful exchange outside situation.			

Figure 6 McCafferty: Performance Chart

WRITE	WRITE	READ	READ	READ
Report factually, comment, draw conclusions, summarise.	*Explain, propose, convey attitude, relationship.*	*Extract gist, find relevant information.*	*Extract detailed information and relate to situation.*	*Follow argument of complex discourse, group connections.*
Can prepare minutes of meetings, report on proposals, progress.	Can prepare planning proposal with comments on pros and cons.	Skim reads effectively and extracts small pieces of information from long texts quickly.	Can evaluate importance and relevance of accurately understood abstracted information.	Can read a series of articles, papers and forms and see argument clearly.
Can report on visits, visitors' situations, decisions with comment.	Can defend, support, oppose a course of action or decision or proposal.	Can find what is relevant, important in wide selection of materials.	Can use files and reference material efficiently and make logical connections.	Can read a file of correspondence and understand whole.
Can prepare briefs for visitors, meetings, describe situation.	Can write effective memos, letters, in reponse to a range of problems.	Can find key words, phrases, concepts and make correct associations.	Can produce accurate information on request from files or reference books.	Can follow argument of newspaper, magazine articles.
Can give information in reply to queries one point at a time.	Can explain problems with own work, give reasons, complain.	Can recognise drift, sort correspondence, articles into topic areas.	Can extract implicit as well as explicit information.	Can follow straightforward chain of reasoning in sequential paragraphs.
Can describe functions of posts, processes, procedures in simple language.	Can make arrangements for meeting, check or cancel appointments.	Can recognise relevance at paragraph level and vary pace accordingly.	Can extract factual but not logical or implied information.	Can understand each point of argument but often fails to see connections.
Can write routine 'standard' letters in answer to simple queries.	Can write 'stock' letters or memos of apology, assurance, promise.	Can cope with short memos or letters but not with anything longer.	Can follow and act correctly upon routine letters, memos, instructions.	Can understand a process or procedure from a description.
Can give personal details or describe job in short phrases.	Can give straightforward directions, instructions in memo or 'standard' format.	Reads at sentence level, digests each sentence before going on to next.	Can work from familiar forms, notices, work sheets.	Can see simple relationships showing cause, effect and simple conditions.
Can fill in form, work sheet, about own work.	Can complete appropriate forms using one verb sentences.	Reads word by word from beginning, cannot predict or vary pace.	Can follow simple instructions, time or place.	Can establish relationship between sentences but treats each sentence individually.
Can complete forms which require one word or simple 'stock phrase' answers.		Reads and digests at simple sentence level – one sentence at a time.		
Can write name and address and a few personal details, some numbers.		Recognises individual words, street names, public signs, shop names.		

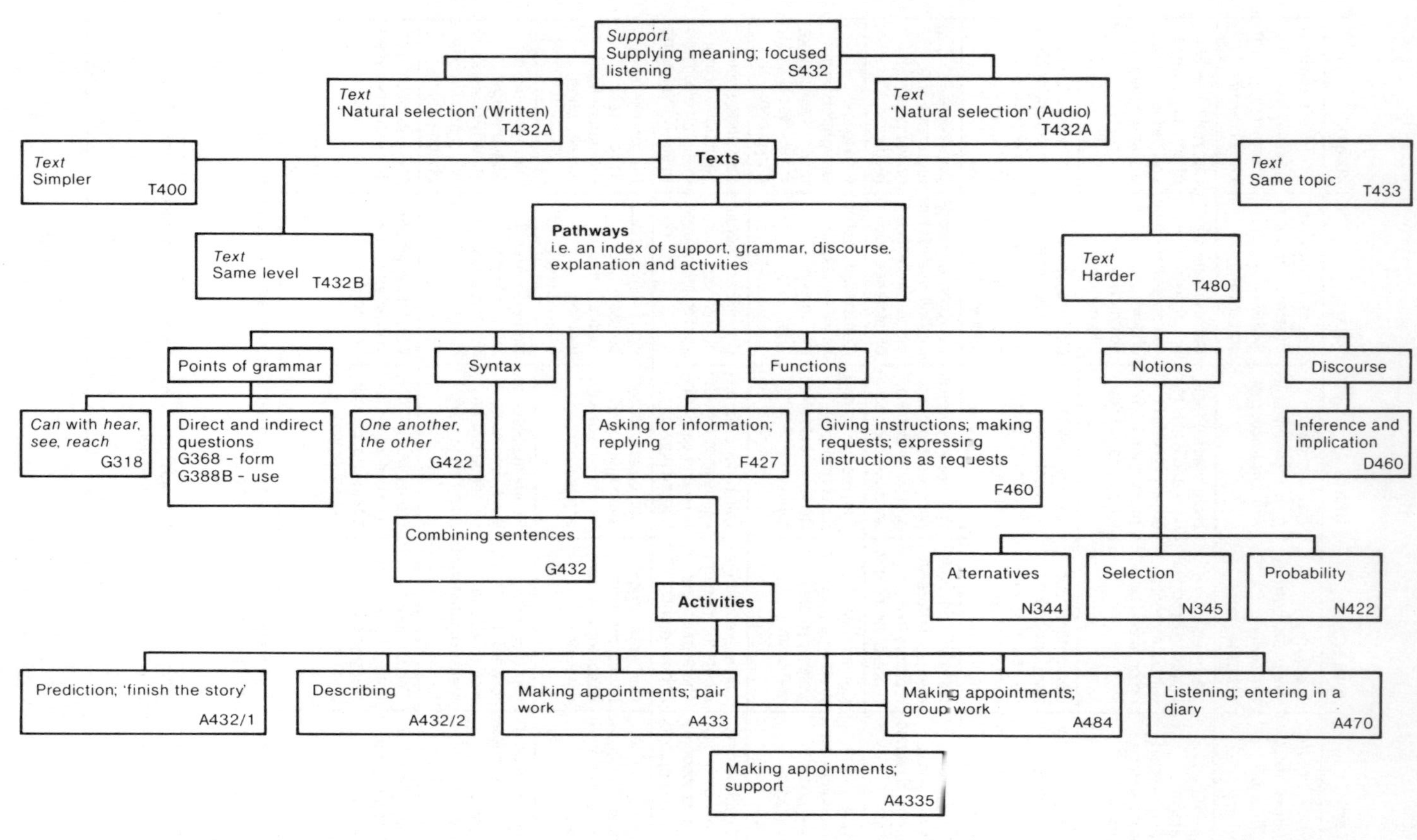

Figure 7 *A sample Network*

> The learner is free to start at any point in the system. One learner may decide that since he is not at all clear what 'functions' are, he would like to start with support material on 'functions'. Another may decide that she cannot understand spoken English well enough to listen to tapes. The starting point is unimportant insofar as wherever the learner starts, a series of 'Pathways' offer suggestions as to what might profitably be done next.
>
> McCafferty (ND: 14)

As the learner is working on the materials in a Network he can consult a helper whenever he wishes. The helper is available to give to the learner whatever help he needs: thus the helper may give advice or information on individual problems or act as a resource to fill in gaps in the materials Network (for example, the 'help cards' may not give the help needed in every case). He may organise pair and group work and other activities where interaction is involved, provide endorsement of both the learner's choice of Pathway and of the learner's own evaluation of progress, and provide a back-up service whenever the learner feels that the system has let him down (McCafferty ND: 23). At some point the learner has to get out of the Network and, if appropriate, move to another. Networks are designed to provide sufficient material for a representative sample of likely users at that level, so there is much too much material for any one learner. But how does the learner know when to move on? A self-evaluation scheme is suggested with the following components.

Progress cards, standard cards which are used for work on a text or explanation, suggest to the learner that he awards himself a score from a five-point scale. The points at the top, middle and bottom of the scale are shown in figure 8. Scores could be entered in a Learner Diary and some total, discovered by trial and error, would indicate that enough work had been done on a particular box.

5	4	3	2	1
Nothing new		Some new language		All new
Nothing I did not know		Some things recalled		Did not know any of what was there
Nothing I could not understand		Some gaps found and plugged		Did not understand
		Understood with help		

Figure 8

5	4	3	2	1
Of course I can do that		*Just!*	*What was that all about?*	

Figure 9

Work on activities would be assessed on a different standard card (see figure 9), again on a five-point scale.

Achievement tests are closely linked to the target box from the Network. These tests could be based on audio, video, print material or on interactions. They would yield a numerical score closely associated with some relevant behaviour – for example, number of lines read, number of words, patterns not understood, number of minutes taken, number of correct responses produced or number of interactions identified correctly. These would either be self-monitored, or monitored by a helper or native speaker (McCafferty ND: 69).

3.1.4 Moray House College, Edinburgh

Note: The scheme described below was in operation in 1983. It is presently under revision.

The Language Skills programme in the Scottish Centre for Education Overseas (SCEO) sets out to achieve three rather different aims within a number of constraints. The aims are:

a) to help course members to improve their English language proficiency;
   - in study skills relevant to the courses they are following,
   - in their use of English in social contexts in the UK,
   - and, in general, to improve their English language models;

b) to help course members to achieve self-direction in their study;
c) to demonstrate self-directed learning as an instructional possibility.

All the participants in this programme are either practising or trainee English language teachers. They come from a wide variety of countries, and consequently of language backgrounds: they have a variety of educational backgrounds and ability levels. These participants are different in certain significant ways from those in the other schemes described here. Firstly, their main purpose is to take a course of English language teacher training. The language improvement aspect of this course is seen by most participants as important in a general way, but few are spontaneously aware of specific language improvement objectives they wish to achieve. Secondly, it is compulsory for them to take part in the language skills course, whereas learners in the other institutions are self-selected. Thirdly, all the SCEO course members regard their competence in the English language as a major qualification for their profession of English language teaching. Consequently, there may be a conflict between their intellectual recognition that their competence can be improved and the threat to their professional *amour propre*.

The self-directed language skills programme begins, ironically, with 30 hours of teacher-directed intensive study of academic writing at the rate of six hours per week over five weeks. It is, we believe, very much easier for learners to discover their language learning needs when they are actively engaged in some aspect of language learning. During this period we try to encourage thought about language learning objectives, partly through workshop tasks and partly through seminars in which the participants discuss possible needs. The students are put into groups of about 15, each with a tutor, and they work on material prepared in SCEO which aims to help students to write coherent, well-shaped academic essays. It also aims to encourage co-operative working, peer and self-assessment, and to initiate the process of language learning needs analysis. The writing materials work requires students to operate individually, then in pairs and then in groups. This way of working helps to dispense with the misunderstanding that individualisation equals isolation. However, co-operative working does not just happen, especially among people who are products of, and employed in highly competitive educational systems. They need to be convinced that it is permissible and that it works; so we make it compulsory for the first five weeks!

The analysis of the students' language learning needs is a relatively lengthy process which is initiated during this intensive course, but continues throughout the first term. At intervals during the intensive phase students are asked to think about their personal language learning/improvement objectives. During the final hour of the first week of study, the students are asked to make a preliminary statement of personal objectives, then during the third week they are asked to reconsider these objectives and a group discussion is held on the general issue of objectives. At the end of the intensive phase we spend three or four class periods carefully considering language needs, and undertaking various exercises, the outcome of which is a contract (see Chapter 6) completed by each student, covering the next two or three weeks. Subsequent contracts are completed by most students without help, though help from tutors and peers is available if it is required.

The language skills programme proper – that is after the termination of the academic writing course – operates within a relatively flexible framework of assessment. Each student must obtain a pass for each term's work. To obtain a pass the students must demonstrate that they have been doing an adequate amount of work on their objectives (checked against the contract and a record of work completed); and they must complete a language skills project, taking about six hours' work.

The options open to students for working towards objectives include both self-directed and tutor-directed learning modes. The self-directed work is organised by the student himself largely through the contract form and is usually based on the self-access resources centres in the College: these house published and locally produced texts and recorded audio and video materials, reference books and various guides and indexes to help students to locate the relevant materials. Tutors are available in the SCEO resource centre for consultation for two hours per week.

Running parallel to the self-directed programme there are two tutor-directed options. The first is a programme concerned with interactive oral skills which offers a simulation or a role play to a proportion of the students each week on a sign-up basis, as an alternative to self-directed work. The second possibility is a continuation of the academic writing course. In addition to the pass awarded for satisfactory work in the language skills course, students get a language proficiency score which is recorded and is one of the assessments which goes towards forming their professional profiles. This test is administered once a term over three terms, and each student is required to take the test at least once, and may take it on all three occasions. Where someone opts to take it more than once the best score obtained is recorded. In practice the students are discouraged from taking the test more than once unless there is a good reason for doing so.

Self-directed learning is exemplified in several ways in the programme:

- The students are free to design their own courses of study through the regular completion of contracts.
- They are free to select or design the ways that the achievement of their selected objectives may be assessed.
- They can decide when to take the language proficiency test.
- Finally they are free to select preferred learning modes and strategies.

3.2 Schemes at school level

Three schemes are described: the Circle Model and the Flower Model, both from Denmark; and the Private Study Model from England.

3.2.1 The Circle Model

This model was developed for use in Danish secondary schools (described to me by Else Lange) some years ago and has certain similarities to McCafferty's Network. It was introduced as one solution to the problems of teaching pupils with a wide range of abilities when streaming was abandoned. It is intended to be a complete system – that is, a system which occupies all the class contact time available – in contrast to partial systems which may be optional extras to the regular class or may be periodic events within the regular class timetable. The Circle Model elegantly captures several principles of self-directed learning; in particular, the learners are offered the choice between working independently of the teacher (alone, in pairs or in groups) or of working

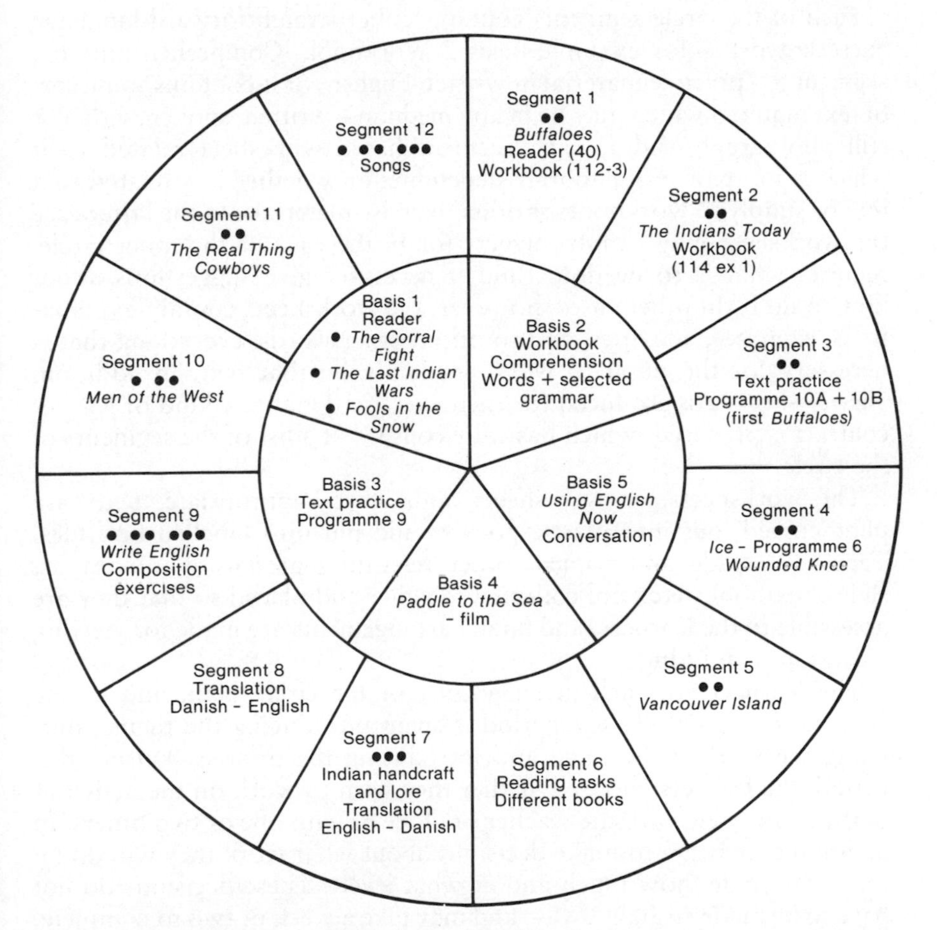

Figure 10 The Circle Model: 'Red Indians'

in a group led by the teacher. In addition they are offered a large range of choices on what to do, all within a guiding framework and all directed towards an external examination.

The presentation of the syllabus is done through a series of themes and the work for each theme is laid out in a circle, which accounts for the name (see figure 10). The work – and the circle – is dividied into two major categories. First, there is a compulsory part which is shown in the inner circle, and labelled Bases 1 to 5. This is work directly related to the examination and it has to be completed by each learner. The outer circle represents a set of choices of various kinds, and at different levels of difficulty indicated by a series of dots. One dot indicates a fairly simple exercise whilst three dots shows a difficult one. The learners can make choices amongst the exercises and there is some choice about how much of the optional work to do.

Each of the circle segments contains either straightforward language exercise work – for example Basis 2 Workbook, Comprehension etc., segment 9 – practice material in written English; or it contains some sort of text material which may be in any medium – written, spoken, video or still photographs/slides. Each segment has a worksheet related to it which is more or less elaborate depending on whether it is related to a text or simply to workbook or other exercise materials. In the latter case the worksheet may simply suggest (or in the case of the inner circle, require) what is to be done, and if necessary give suggestions about how to do it. In other cases, however, the worksheets contain explanations, exercises, activities, and so on; in other words, everything that is necessary for the pupil to work profitably on that text. In addition, answer sheets are produced for each exercise. Finally, a kind of learner contract is prepared, which basically consists of a list of the segments of the circle.

The worksheets, answer sheets and, where appropriate, texts are photocopied, put into plastic pockets and put into labelled box files. Tapes are made and copied, other relevant materials, photographs, slides, textbooks etc., are collected together and placed so that they are accessible to the learners, and finally arrangements are made for viewing video tapes and films.

The learners are each given a copy of the circle plan, and of the contract form. One lesson period is spent introducing the theme, outlining the work to be done and introducing the options. During this period, the learners choose whether they wish to work on the activities of the inner circle with the teacher or alone or with one or two others. In addition they begin to make decisions about what work they will do on the outer circle, how much and at what levels. These decisions do not have to be made straight away, and may take a week or two to complete. They are then recorded on the contract forms.

The whole class begins together on Basis 1 which is an introduction to the theme, often in the form of a short story or a film, but after that the class splits up into various groups. One group will be working with the teacher on Bases 2 to 4, while the others will be working individually or in groups. Though all the learners have to complete the work of the inner circle by the end of the time allocated for the theme, it does not all have to be completed before the optional work is begun. Some of it (varying from theme to theme) is seen as a prerequisite for the outer circle work, and so this has to be completed first. Thereafter learners can work on what they wish.

Else Lange, who described the scheme, made the following comments about its preparation and operation:

- The preparation work is immense. It can be reduced to some degree by co-operating with other teachers over each theme. (Additionally, themes prepared in the past can be used again, and it may be possible to exchange themes among teachers.)
- Oral work is more difficult to organise than reading and writing and tends to get neglected.
- There have been very few disciplinary problems with pupils using these schemes. The learners seem to like the system and work very hard in it.
- It does not seem to be restricted to older – or younger – learners. It has been used with learners from 11 to 17.

3.2.2 The Flower Model

The approach used by Leni Dam, of the Karleslunde Skole, Denmark, assumes from the beginning that the pupils are responsible for their own learning. She has developed this approach for use with full classes (that is, groups of 20–30), and the class she describes in her papers (1982, 1983a, 1983b) was a fifth year (12–13 years old), with 25 pupils consisting of 16 girls and nine boys. The children, who are in their first year of English, have four hours per week of English, one two hour period and two one hour ones. Most of the pupils come from non-academic backgrounds, and a lower proportion than average of the children from the catchment area progress to the Gymnasium (upper secondary school).

The key elements are:

- Pupils work out their own needs and interests.
- They arrange their own syllabuses deriving from their own needs.
- The learners make decisions about what they are going to work on and how they are going to work.
- They make contracts with themselves and the teacher covering the work they have decided to do.

The model of language education on which this is based is represented as a series of 'petals' of a flower, from which the model takes its name (see figure 11).

At the very start of the course the learners are faced with the questions: 'Why do you learn English?' and 'What do you intend to do with the language?' These questions are discussed between the teacher and the pupils, and among the pupils themselves in groups. This discussion forms the basis for the learners deciding on their needs for the language.

The actual learning of English during this initial period is based on language material brought along by the pupils. It consists of stickers, stamps, children's books, magazines, jokes, phrases recorded on trips abroad and so on. The children all have copies of the *Oxford Picture*

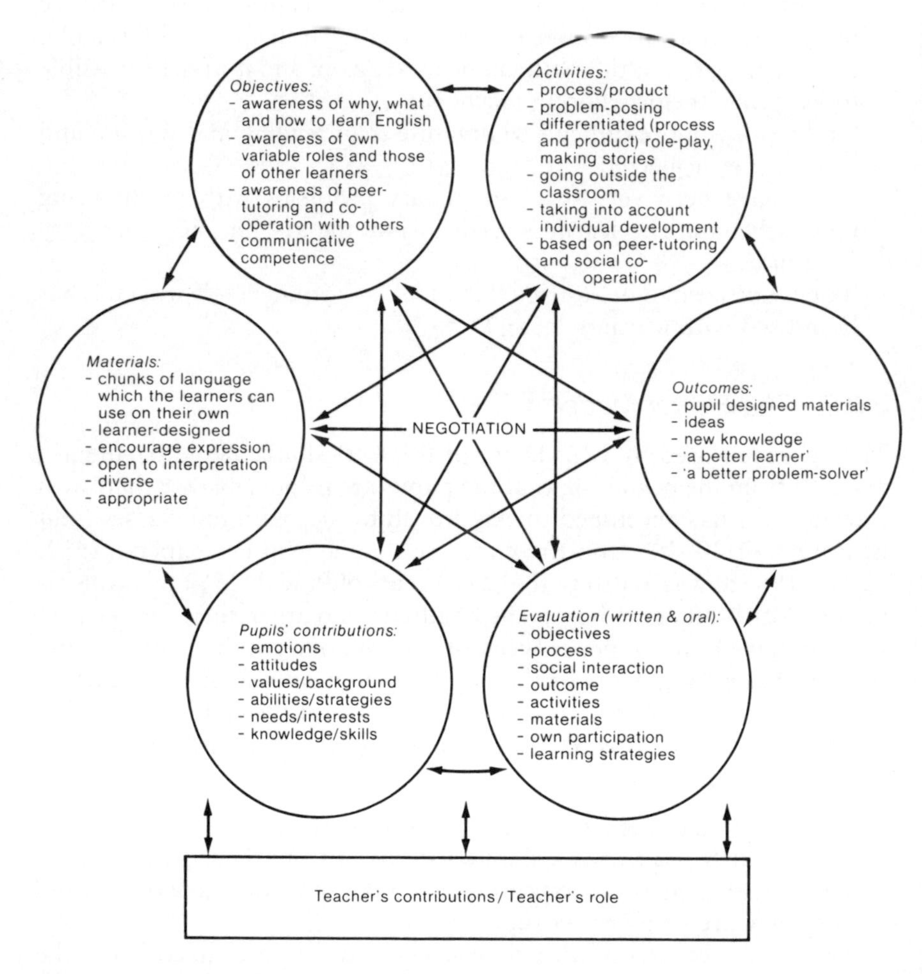

Figure 11 The Flower Model

Dictionary, and there are a few copies of course books as part of the learning resources, but no book is used as an English text. They are not taught grammar, but in co-operation with the teacher they work out posters of elementary grammatical rules. These hang on the walls of the classroom for the learners to check grammatical problems when they arise.

Early on in the course the teacher discusses a simple model of language use with the children (see figure 12).

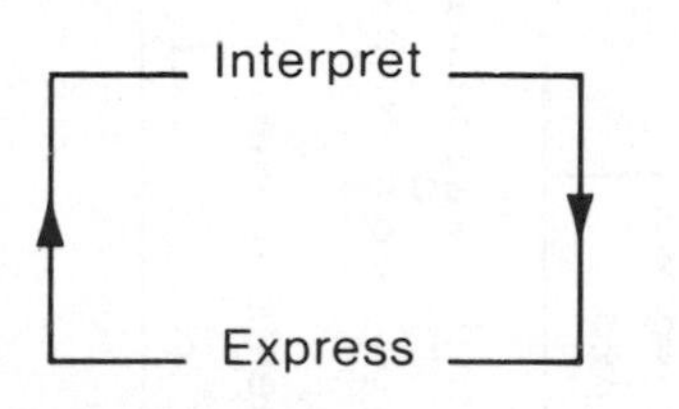

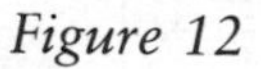

Figure 12

Then the children are given a list of suggested activities based on this model.

Texts

- read a text
- find headings/pictures to go with the text
- write a new text (another pupil)

(A possible development would be to combine the two texts.)

- make a list of catchwords to a text
- make a summary of the text from the catchwords
- let another pupil make/write a new text

- mix a cut-up text
- put it in order
- find headings / make drawings / find pictures
- write a new text (a new pupil)
- dramatise
- write down the play

(In the same way the following activities can be expanded:
- hypothesising/predicting/suggesting
- translating text into poems, slogans, single words
- translations.)

Figure 13 Activities/tasks

English/Period: Name: Beunce

Subject/what to achieve: School

1. Write to people in a English school.
2. We want to get some information about the English school.
3. We/I will write, spell, talk better

Date	Task/activity	Materials	Comments
23.9.83	Writing letter – make some questions to a letter read in "This is GB Life at School."	dictionaries, a book about English schools	Where are the "questions"?
26.9.83	Today are we going to have a look at a film called: "At school with Mark and Dawn" or "A Stage School"		Before watching the film decide what you're looking for – be prepared to take notes.

Homework: For: Monday 26th September
* read "British Isles", English School", and "This is GB Life at School".
I have read in: "English School" only the first page.

Teacher's comments to plan:
* see separate comments

English/Period: Name: mitat Group 1

Subject/what to achieve: family life. we will be better (to write) English. at writing

Date	Task/activity	Materials	Comments
23/9	Describing a family life	this is GB (life with the family) Page 9.15	Where are your examples? OR was Karin the only one to do the writing? What have you done in order to be better at writing?
26/9 – 26/9	We was going to write a example's in family life. We have writing a example's		

Homework: * read page 9 and 15 in this is GB.
*read page 14 breakfast

Teacher's comments to plan:
* see separate comments

Figure 14

In addition a work sheet is introduced over one period which the teacher has filled in. In groups the pupils try out various activities and report to the rest of the class: Were they good or bad? Why? What can they be used for? The results are written on big posters and put on to the wall. In the next stage, the teacher specifies the topic, but the groups decide on the subject matter. For the topic 'England', for example, groups chose things like English schools, family life, English food and so on. Besides deciding on the content, pupils also have to decide 'what to achieve', that is, they have to specify their objectives. Leni Dam comments that they find this very difficult and need a lot of help. The help is given largely through comments written on the worksheets. Finally, after some months of English, pupils are asked to work out what they wish to achieve over the next 20 lessons (five weeks' work). Each pupil writes down what he wishes to achieve in this period of time, and groups are formed on the basis of these lists. Worksheets are completed and agreed in the groups, and then work begins. (See figure 14.)

Regular evaluation is a key part of the process, encouraging pupils to think about what they have been doing, what the successes were, what problems they came up against and how they might solve them. In this scheme the overall language learning aim is the same as for other teachers in Denmark – to develop the communicative competence of the pupils – but in addition, here the pupils are being helped towards autonomy in their learning. Finally, there is ample evidence from the pupils' evaluations that they enjoy the experience, that they believe they are learning a lot of English and that they are in the process of achieving autonomy. For example, in response to the question, 'How do you see your own role in the "teaching of English"?' one pupil answered, 'Almost all the time I have found out myself what I wanted to do. Only a few times have I not been able to do this.' Another responded, 'I think that I have tried to do as much as possible, but I only did that when I started doing something, but when I find something difficult, I start playing the fool but I can't help doing that.' They were then asked whether they found their own work satisfactory, and to say why it was or why it was not. One pupil replied, 'I think it was satisfactory almost all the time because I think that working with English is fun and when there is something I think is interesting I can pull myself together.' The children were then asked to say what activities and/or materials they used and why. A selection of responses is given in figure 15.

»»→

Activities	Why
I have played drama	Learn new words
Worked at the book "Come along 7th Form"	Something new to work with
Heard "Alice in Wonderland"	Exciting to listen to real English
Made a play "Badcrew"	Learn new words
Read a book "John Crump" on tape	Because I learnt new words
"Aladdin"	Many good new words
PLAY LOTTERY	LEARNED NEW WORDS AND DESCRIBED THINGS IN ENGLISH.

Figure 15

3.2.3 The Private Study Model

Frequently, self-instructional systems are used as adjuncts to conventional, teacher-led class systems. In a sense, of course, this has always been the case, since homework assignments are examples of self-instruction. However, the kinds of schemes I have in mind here are those which are classroom – or institution – based and where the learners are frequently given a degree of choice over what they will do, and maybe, how they will do it. Cross (1980) describes one such scheme operating with 14–16-year-old pupils in an English comprehensive school; the learners, who have opted to continue with foreign language learning, are taught in mixed ability groups for two complete half days per week. Twenty-five per cent of that time is allocated to 'private study' sessions, and twenty-five per cent to pair and small group role-play activities. During the private study sessions the learners may work on any aspect of the language which they choose, they 'are able to follow up an interest, to remedy a weakness, to forge ahead into new areas of language work, or they may read books in the foreign language.' (Cross 1980: 112)

The learners can work individually or in pairs, and they have free access to cassette players and headsets. The private study materials are mainly produced by the modern language teachers in the school, and Cross claims that each booklet takes only about an hour to write. Most booklets have an accompanying cassette giving a native speaker model for all the target language examples; explanations are written in English. The topics include a review of basic structures, suitable particularly for weaker learners; grammatical points dealt with in a traditional way; and a set of booklets dealing with selected notions and functions. Each booklet contains exercises and suggests suitable communicative activities to be carried out with a partner or a teacher. One example that Cross gives is a booklet that was designed for a pupil who, just before he was due to go to France to stay with a host family, realised that he did not know how to carry out 'small talk' at table. He wanted to be able to compliment, to praise, to criticise and to refuse, politely. In addition he wanted information on the customs and habits of French families so that he would know what to expect, and also, he would know what his host family expected of him.

Some examples of Cross's booklets and their coverage in terms of functions and notions are given in figure 16.

Topic	*Functions*	*Notions*
self, family	exchanging information	age, appearance
past tense diary	narrating past activities	time
large shop	volition seeking information	location

Figure 16

3.3 Conclusion

The point was made at the beginning of the chapter that unless we were clear about the context of self-instruction, it was not possible to say anything very useful about suitable materials. Consequently, the main purpose of this chapter has been to provide several examples of self-instructional systems in order to provide contexts for the discussion in the following chapters of the various ways of facilitating and supporting learners.

4 Materials for self-instruction

The major questions addressed in this chapter are:

- What are the sources of self-instructional materials?
- How can existing materials be adapted for self-instructional use? An example of the adaptation of a unit of material is offered and discussed.
- How do self-instructional materials differ from other materials? This section lists and examines the specific design features required in materials to make them suitable for self-instruction.

There are three sources of materials for self-instruction: authentic texts used directly by the learner; commercially available courses and other materials, used as they are or after adaptation; and materials which are specially written by the staff of the institution. These sources are obviously not exclusive in that any learner's programme, or any Network (see figure 7 in Chapter 3) may consist of all three kinds of material.

4.1 Authentic texts used directly by the learner

Where a self-instructional system is catering for learners with very specific requirements in language learning – for example, in the case of Liz Pearson, whose needs were described in Chapter 1; or maybe in the case of a chemical engineer who wishes to read scientific articles in Russian – it is frequently most effective to base the learning materials on relevant authentic texts (at least after the establishment of the basic structure and vocabulary of the language). In addition there is a growing movement among language teaching practitioners towards authenticity in textual materials. (Authenticity is variously defined, but a common theme in many definitions concerns textual materials which have not been prepared for language teaching.) CRAPEL have for a long time had an ideological commitment to the use of authentic texts in language learning materials, and indeed, they use *only* authentic texts. Riley (1981a) makes out a powerful case for the use of authentic documents. He notes that this makes it possible to meet learners' needs accurately and economically since by choosing documents of the type that the learner encounters or will encounter in her professional area, she is able to concentrate on their lexical, grammatical, functional and interactional characteristics without wasting time on irrelevant problems. In this way the use of authentic documents favours the development of individual learning strategies. The tutor's role in using authentic documents is *not* to attempt to acquire the learner's specialised knowledge (which is difficult where there is one learner and virtually impossible where there are several with different specialities), but to aim to help the learners to develop study techniques which can be applied to any document. This is an elegant solution to a problem which has troubled teachers of language for specific purposes for a long time – the fact that they often do not understand the content of the texts. The acceptance that the learner possesses the specialist knowledge of the content while the tutor has the specialist knowledge of language study techniques can lead to a collaborative approach to learning and help to accelerate the trend towards autonomy. However, it is necessary for the learners to accept that the teacher may not have specialist knowledge of the content, and the occasional learner's inability to accept this may lead to tensions. Techniques which can be used by learners to exploit authentic texts are described in Appendix C(I).

4.2 Commercially available materials*

The big advantage of commercial materials is their convenience and their variety. They are immediately available and there is a wide choice. The disadvantages include the fact that commercial materials are rarely designed for self-instruction, that they are expensive, especially if the materials are being used selectively – that is, if only two or three units of a course are in regular use – and that they are copyright, which prevents them from being copied for students. Many modern publications claim to be suitable for self-instruction, but what this sometimes means is that they have an answer key, and perhaps some notes on the answers. Whilst these are necessary features of self-instructional materials, they are clearly not all that is required. Commercial courses, then, whilst offering a ready supply of available materials, do not offer a complete solution to providing materials for self-instruction. Some such materials are, of course, usable as they stand, and others are usable after adaptation. This raises the problem of how to distinguish those materials which are usable from the rest, and the most convenient way of doing this is to

* The copying of published materials is not normally allowed under copyright legislation unless permission has been previously obtained from the publisher. For example, cutting up published material to make worksheets etc. is permissible, but photocopying from books is not. If you are in any doubt, you should get in touch with the relevant publisher.

evaluate the materials using appropriate criteria. Possible criteria that could be used for this are suggested below under the heading of *Specific design features* (4.3.1).

4.2.1 Adapting materials for self-instruction

Adaptation is used here in the obvious sense – as a process of changing existing (probably commercial) materials to make them more suitable for self-instruction. This usually involves making several additions to the materials so that they will meet the minimum specifications for self-instructional materials. This adaptation assumes an autonomous learner, since materials suitable for autonomous use can be used in other formats, whereas the reverse is not usually the case.

The process of adaptation is illustrated by Unit 19 from *Task Listening* (Blundell and Stokes 1981). The adapted unit is presented first and it is followed by an account of the adaptations that were made, and why they are thought necessary.

Task Listening Unit 19: Flat hunting (adapted for self-instructional use)

Objectives

- To give practice in listening for details and listening for gist from a conversation between two people;
- To build passive vocabulary of terms concerned with accommodation.

Requirements

- To achieve at least 80 per cent correct answers in the comprehension questions.

BEFORE LISTENING

First read the questions below. Do not answer them yet. *Next* read the passage, and look out for the answers to the questions. After you have read the passage, answer the questions. These activities will help you to think about the topic of flat hunting, and give you explanations of some of the words and phrases used in the listening passage.

Work suggestions. Work with a friend. Check one another on these meanings *after* you have read the passage.

1 Look out for these words and phrases. You can find their meanings when you read the passage. *Do not* use a dictionary yet.
   a) A single room ....
   b) A double room ....
   c) A bedsitter ....
   d) A self-contained flat ....
2 Satisfy yourself that you understand what the following phrases mean *after* you have read the passage.
   a) that's out
   b) that's hopeless } See notes 1 and 2 which follow the passage.
3 The passage uses some *abbreviations* (part of a word to stand for whole word: e.g. = for example; etc. = et cetera, and so on).
   H & C water ....
   CH .... (This one is difficult, see note 3 which follows the passage.)
   £50 p.w. ....
   £200 p.c.m. ....
   (*Note:* If you cannot understand a word or phrase ask a friend. Use a dictionary to check any guesses you are not certain about.)

FINDING ACCOMMODATION

Coming to Britain to study is very exciting but you must find good accommodation quickly so that you can live comfortably. Many students worry about their accommodation; this makes them unhappy and it affects their study.

There are many ways of finding accommodation. Most universities and colleges have an *Accommodation Officer* who will help students to find accommodation. Sometimes though, students have special needs which the Accommodation Officer cannot help with. For example, married students may want a self-contained flat with one or two bedrooms, a sitting room and kitchen and bathroom. Or a student may wish to share a flat with others. One way of finding special accommodation is to go to a flat agency which will have a list of flats to let; another is to look regularly at the *Accommodation Vacant* section of the local newspaper.

Advertisements for flats and rooms are written in a special way and you will have to learn this kind of English or you will not understand them. Firstly there are words and phrases used to describe accommodation. The words *single* and *double* are used a lot. A '*single room*' doesn't mean just one room! It means a room for one person. You will be able to guess what a '*double room*' means. A '*bedsitter*' is a word which has been formed from two other words – a *bedroom* and a *sitting room*. This produced 'bed sitting room' which has become '*bedsitter*', or sometimes just '*bedsit*'. '*Self-contained*' is a word which you could not work out from its parts; it means a flat with all of the necessary facilities such as bathroom and kitchen. If a flat is not self-contained you will have to share one or more of these with other people.

Advertisements use a lot of abbreviations and so you need to learn what these mean. The reason for many of these abbreviations is to reduce the cost of advertising in newspapers. Advertisements are charged by the line, so the shorter the words, the cheaper the advert. *H & C water* is important in a flat, especially if you like to wash , and think it is too cold in Britain to use only cold water. You need heating too, and so *CH* may be important to you. It can be expensive to run, though, and so some people prefer fires in each room. It is important to know what the rent of the flat is because most people have a limit on what they can spend. £50 p.w. may look the same as £200 p.c.m. but you need to be careful about whether the rent is for a calendar month or for a lunar month; that is whether you pay the same for February (which has 28 days) as you do for May (which has 31). These are calendar months. Each lunar month has four weeks.

Finally, some adverts mention special likes or dislikes. Nowadays, many adverts say *Non-smoker* so if you are a smoker, that's out – unless you are willing to give up smoking. Sometimes you get strange comments like 'prefer someone away on Sundays'. If you are a student from overseas living in Britain, that's hopeless; you cannot promise to be away each Sunday so you could not take that flat.

Any problems? Check meanings with your friends. If you are stuck, use a dictionary.

Note 1 That's out = that is out: an idiom meaning that it is not possible. It is no good.
Note 2 That's hopeless: similar to 'that's out' but stronger. = That's totally impossible.
Note 3 CH = Central Heating: heat supplied from radiators which are heated by a central boiler.

LISTENING

Before listening read the comments and questions below. Answer the questions and check the questions with a friend.

Background

Rod and Helen meet in the college common room. They are friends. Rod has recently got married and he is looking for a flat for his wife and himself. There is a limit on the amount of money he wants to spend on the rent. The flat must be near the city centre because he hasn't got a car.

Before you listen

What are you listening for?

1 Look at the tasks on page 38 in the Student's Book. What have you got to do?
   a) ....
   b) ....
   c) ....
2 What is the best order to do them in?
   First .... Second: .... Third: ....
   (Check your answers with a friend. There are suggested answers in the note below.*)

*Suggested answers
1 List the advantages and disadvantages of the houses and flats etc.
   – Tick the one Rod chooses.
   – Answer the questions at the foot of the page.
2 First: (c) Second: (a) Third: (b)

19 Flat hunting

Listening

List the advantages and disadvantages of the houses, flats etc. advertised. Tick the one chosen.
Answer the questions.

Advantages *Disadvantages*

FLAT & HOUSE RENTALS

ABINGDON Road, single attic bedsitter and separate small kitchen £38 and £40 deposit, references. Tel. Oxford 774159

ACCOMMODATION Kennington, suit non-smoking person. Tel. Oxford 739676 preferably 6.30–7.30 p.m.

AVAILABLE immediately. – Exceptionally attractive well appointed Cotswold House in isolated position 11 miles Oxford, 2 double bedrooms with bathrooms and dressing rooms ensuite, single bedroom, study, drawing room with dining area, large kitchen with laundry off, garden, car-port, stabling etc., long let preferred, £150 pcm. Tel. Witney 2554

AVAILABLE SOON, Furnished Flat, suitable young couple. – Tel. Oxford 40414

BEDSITTING Room available now for lady, Summertown, limited use of kitchen, central heating, h and c water, prefer someone away on Sunday.–Tel. Oxford 55898

BEDSIT £14; Flat £28. Cottage £35.– Tel. Oxford 63785.

ROOM IN shared House, £25 pw, central.– Tel. Oxford 724261

What kind of accommodation do these people really want?

For how many people?..............................

Number of bedrooms?..............................

Maximum rent?..............................

How far from city centre?..............................

Anything else?..............................

Figure 17

Listening instructions

Listen to the recording and answer the questions in the Student's Book. Check your answers:
- with a friend; (Are your answers the same? If not listen again.)
- in the answer key in the Teacher's Book.

Listening advice

Do *not* try to understand everything you hear. Listen for relevant information; do not worry about the rest.

Try listening straight through two or three times first. See how much of the task you can do. Then use the stop and rewind keys to check your answers. If you are really stuck, follow the tapescript while you are listening.

After you have done the exercise, use the tapescript to check on parts of the recording which you could not understand.

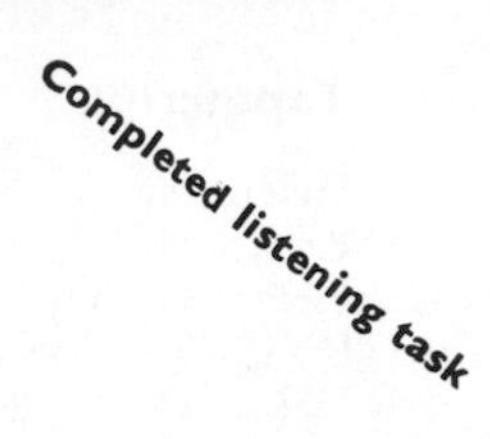

19 Flat hunting

Listening

List the advantages and disadvantages of the houses, flats etc. advertised. Tick the one chosen.
Answer the questions.

Advantages	**FLAT & HOUSE RENTALS**	*Disadvantages*
central	**ABINGDON** Road, single attic bedsitter and separate small kitchen £38 and £40 deposit, references. Tel. Oxford 774159	single
	ACCOMMODATION Kennington, suit non-smoking person. Tel. Oxford 739676 preferably 6.30-7.30 p.m.	for non-smoker, not very central
available immediately	**AVAILABLE** immediately. – Exceptionally attractive well appointed Cotswold House in isolated position 11 miles Oxford, 2 double bedrooms with bathrooms and dressing rooms ensuite, single bedroom, study, drawing room with dining area, large kitchen with laundry off, garden, car-port, stabling etc., long let preferred, £150 pcm. Tel. Witney 2554	11 miles from Oxford
available soon, suit young couple	**AVAILABLE SOON**, Furnished Flat, suitable young couple. – Tel. Oxford 40414	furnished
	BEDSITTING Room available now for lady, Summertown, limited use of kitchen, central heating, h and c water, prefer someone away on Sunday.–Tel. Oxford 55898	for lady
reasonable price	**BEDSIT** £14; Flat £28. ✓ Cottage £35.– Tel. Oxford 63785.	
central	**ROOM IN** shared House, £25 pw, central.– Tel. Oxford 724261	just one room

What kind of accommodation do these people really want?

For how many people? 2

Number of bedrooms? more than 1

Maximum rent? £30 per week

How far from city centre? not more than 2 or 3 miles

Anything else? must be allowed to smoke

Figure 18

Tapescript

Helen: Hi.
Rod: Hi.
Helen: Gosh, you're not still looking for a flat are you?
Rod: Yes. I've been looking for six weeks now. It's driving me mad you know.
Helen: Do you want any help?
Rod: Yes you'd be a great help actually.
Helen: Let's have a look at the newspaper together.
Rod: Yes.
Helen: What about that one 'Abingdon Road, single attic bedsitter'...er...
Rod: No single's no good because there's two of us you see.
Helen: Yes? OK. Have you ...Have you... got a limit as to how much you want to spend?
Rod: Yes. It mustn't be more than £30 a week (OK) I think that's about the maximum you know.
Helen: Right. OK. What about the next one then?
Rod: 'Accommodation Kennington' (Yes) 'suit non-smoking person'. That's no good because Liz smokes so...
Helen: Does she?
Rod: Yes.
Helen: I thought she'd stopped.
Rod: Well she tried to give up but you know like everything else she tries it for a couple of days and that's it.
Helen: Yes? Well maybe you could persuade her to give up (Yes) ... still Kennington's not very central is it.
Rod: No and see I haven't got a car and it's much too far to cycle.
Helen: Right.
Rod: ...erm... 'available immediately'. God this sounds good! Look at that!
Helen: 'Exceptionally attractive, well-appointed Cotswold house.' Gosh yes! Oh but look, it's eleven miles from Oxford. (Mm). Yes. That'd be hopeless. How far do you reckon you could cycle, I mean eleven miles?
Rod: I reckon about, no, two or three miles is the limit really.
Helen: Yes?
Rod: I'm getting old you know.
Helen: Oh that's out then. Oh but it does look fantastic, doesn't it?
Rod: 'Available soon. Furnished flat. Suitable young couple.'
Helen: Ah. That's nice.
Rod: Ah. Furnished. Must be unfurnished.
Helen: Why?
Rod: She's got all that old stuff of her mother's you know.
Helen: You've got to use that?
Rod: Yes we have really.
Helen: That's no good then.
Rod: So that's out.
Helen: 'Bedsitting room available now for lady.' Well that'd be all right for Liz but not for you.
Rod: No ... that's no good.
Helen: ...erm... 'Prefer someone away on Sunday.' What a funny idea!
Rod: Mm. 'Bedsit £14. Flat £28.' Mm. That's a possibility. What's this 'Room in shared house £25 per week, central.'
Helen: Well it's central... central.

Rod: No good though.
Helen: Why?
Rod: It's just a room you see. We need something self-contained.
Helen: Yes. It could be quite a big one though. Still there are two of you aren't there.
Rod: Yes (Yes) I think that that ...erm... early one is the only possibility really.
Helen: Yes. Well give them a ring see what they say.
Rod: Yes I'm getting sick of this, shall we have a cup of coffee?
Helen: Yes let's finish.

Figure 19

Background to the adaptation of materials

The general purpose of adaptations carried out for self-instruction is to provide the learner with the kind of help, advice and encouragement given by a teacher using the same material in a classroom. The procedure that I have used to adapt the materials follows this rationale. That is, I first decided on how I would prepare the material for use in the classroom – using the Teacher's Book and my own ideas – and then I wrote out the presentation in such a way that it could be understood by the learners.

The adaptation has provided some extra information and advice. The extra information is contained in the reading passage, and there is a brief summary of the listening text. There is advice on reading and listening strategies and on working procedures. The intention of the reading passage and the preliminary questions is primarily to alert learners to important vocabulary items, idioms and phrases, and to provide:

- an appropriate 'set induction' in that it gets learners thinking about the topic, and may arouse their interest;
- contextualised vocabulary items, idioms and phrases which occur in the listening passage and which will probably cause difficulty for some learners;
- some background cultural information on the topic which will enable learners to understand more fully what is going on;
- practice in techniques for discovering word meaning (for example, guessing from context, spotting synonyms etc.).

The advice preliminary to reading is intended to:

- alert learners to important vocabulary items, idioms etc., and suggest that they attempt to discover the meaning from the context;
- suggest strategies for approaching the reading (and to a lesser extent,

the listening) passage (for example, 'Look out for these words and phrases. You can find their meanings when you read the passage. Do *not* use a dictionary yet.')
- alert learners to particularly difficult items (for example, 'that's out') and tell them where they can find the meaning.

The work preliminary to listening consists of a brief note on the content of the listening passage to contextualise it and to provide information important to understanding the listening passage. It also consists of two questions which are intended to alert the learners to the tasks which the textbook requires of them, so making as sure as possible that they know what to do. In addition it endeavours to get learners thinking about the work strategies they will adopt; in this case the best order in which to tackle the tasks.

Finally, scattered through the adaptation there are simple pieces of advice about how to work. Thus learners are sometimes advised to work by themselves (for example, 'Listen by yourself first and answer the questions by yourself.') On other occasions, they are advised to work with a friend and to compare answers. They are given simple advice about listening (for example, 'Do *not* try to understand everything you hear ...') And finally, they are told where they can get confirmation of their answers. In this case they are directed to the Teacher's Book. In other cases an answer key would have to be provided, that is, written by the tutors.

4.2.2 Presentation of adapted materials

Materials which have been adapted for self-instructional use in, for example, a self-access resource centre, need to be packaged in appropriate ways for the users. This packaging might include providing a check-list of activities, the physical division of the book into its constituent units and presenting each unit in a plastic folder.

Carroll *et al.* (1971) recommend the preparation of a check-list of activities for use with each unit of a course book recommended to students. The check-list includes the relevant cassette number for each recorded exercise, a list of appropriate written and oral drills, exercises or other activities with references to the pages of the course book and to any related work book or supplementary sheets the staff of the institution have prepared, a statement of the appropriate pre-test and post-test procedures, and suggested methods and techniques for learning such as practice with a partner or in a group, or dictation with a tutor, a peer or a tape at such and such a point in the programme. The check-list, then, effectively co-ordinates the work of the student and gives instructions, help and advice about using the materials.

Another consideration in presentation is how to make a single book available to several students at once. One solution is to cut course books up into their constituent units and put the pages into plastic folders and/or laminate them in plastic. Additional materials – supplements necessary or desirable for self-instructors, tests and answer sheets, and the check-list mentioned above – can be included in the folder. The resulting package then becomes an independent unit which can be indexed separately and can cater for the needs of several students (Ganserhoff 1979:64).

4.3 Materials written specially for self-instruction

Specially written materials have the advantage that they are relevant to the needs of the learners for whom they are written and that they are specifically designed for self-instruction. In many of the systems designed in Chapter 3, an important function of the tutor is to prepare materials to meet the special needs of learners within the system as the needs emerge (Cambridge, CRAPEL), or to prepare materials to meet the objectives set up by the system (The British Council, The Circle Model). The disadvantage of writing materials specially for learners is the amount of time and effort that it requires. The prospect of stocking a self-access resource centre from scratch entirely with self-prepared materials is very daunting. It is also unnecessary, since some commercial materials are suitable, especially if they are presented in the ways described above.

However, it will usually be necessary for some, and perhaps quite a lot, of the materials to be prepared by the staff of the institution. Views of writers vary as to how major a task this is. Cross (1980:115) is encouraging about how easy it is. His material is handwritten in exercise books and he says that such materials 'can be written in a few inspired minutes. Certainly I would not expect to spend more than one hour in producing at least the major part of the booklet.' Else Lange, on the other hand, in describing the Circle Model, describes the preparatory work as 'immense'. A workable compromise which is widely used is to begin a self-access resource system by stocking it with published material, and whatever written and spoken texts are available in the institution; and preparing specifically relevant materials and adaptations either as the need arises, or when the tutors have the time. Under this compromise, the setting up time is still lengthy, but the centre can operate in limited spheres long before this.

There is no magic formula for the preparation of self-instructional materials, nor for the adaptation of commercial materials, merely the need to keep in mind that when they are in use there may be no readily available teacher to administer, supplement or explain them. Consequently, the materials themselves should ideally contain the help and information which a teacher would supply. Since there is no teacher to give information on how to use the materials, they must be fully explicit in a language understood by the learner. And since there is no teacher to give information on meanings, grammatical information and so on, these must be predicted and supplied. Similarly, since we cannot assume that a teacher will be available to give help with monitoring the learner's performance, the learner herself must do this using answers and explanations supplied in the materials. Moreover, since there may be no-one to give direction in the organisation of the work – such matters as the order of the units to be worked on, the pacing of the work, the timing of the work, the intensity of the work, the combination of various materials – then the materials themselves either must have such organisation built into them, or they must provide advice and help for the learner to make decisions for herself.

4.3.1 Specific design features

Self-instructional materials should have all the features good language *teaching* materials have – interest, variety, clarity and so on. However in addition they should also contain the following:

- a clear statement of objectives;
- meaningful language input;
- exercise materials and activities;
- flexibility of materials;
- learning instructions;
- language learning advice;
- feedback and tests;
- advice about record keeping;
- reference materials;
- indexing;
- motivational factors;
- advice about progression.

Clear objectives

It is important for learners to be clear about the objectives of the learning unit they are tackling, partly on the common sense grounds that it is a great deal easier to do something if you know clearly what it is that you are trying to do, but also to help learners to develop responsibility for their own learning. The first stage of this is to be aware of the objectives of what one is currently learning, as a preparation to making decisions oneself. The second stage is to assess the objectives of the materials against one's own purposes for learning the language. The final stage is to specify one's own objectives and to seek materials to meet them. In addition to this a clear statement of objectives is useful for the purpose of indexing the materials unit by unit for use in a self-access resource.

Meaningful language input

In autonomous learning (and maybe in other learning modes) a major part of the language input will come from the materials. (Other input will come from competent speakers of the language, tutors, and other learners.) The language input from the materials must obviously be comprehensible for it to be useful. In part, this concerns the linguistic level of the material *vis-à-vis* the learners' level, but it also concerns the degree of support supplied to learners to help them to discover meaning. This support includes such things as illustrations, transcriptions of spoken texts, summaries in simpler language of both written and spoken texts, translations, glossaries and explanations of all kinds.

Exercise materials and activities

An important task in preparing or evaluating materials is to ensure that there are sufficient activities and exercises to enable a group of learners to achieve the objectives of the unit. There should also be reasonable variety in these activities, first to cater for different types of learner by providing different paths to the same learning objective – perhaps simply by having choices of spoken versus written exercises for structural or functional objectives; and second to maintain interest among all learners by using a wide selection of different exercises and activities.

Another factor to be considered is the feasibility of the activities for self-instructional use. An important question in this context concerns the amount of organisation which practice activities may require. Activities which require several participants and elaborate materials may not be readily organised by learners themselves. A few of these kinds of activities can be set up by a tutor, but course materials which have many such activities may be less suitable for self-instruction.

Flexibility of materials

Conflicts can arise between one principle of individualisation – the accommodation of the various learning styles and strategies of learners – and the rigidity of some materials which 'instruct' learners to perform tasks in particular ways. It is, of course, possible for the learner to ignore the instructions and perform the task according to his own preferences, however, this may risk the censure of a tutor; '... If the student is "caught" by the teacher not working according to the instructions he may be made to feel that he is cheating in some way, or not working correctly' (Sturtridge 1982:11).

Learning instructions

Intelligible learning instructions are desirable for all materials, but they are crucial for self-instructional ones. Intelligibility may mean using the mother tongue, and certainly means that the instructions must be clear and simple (whatever the language used) so that all learners can follow them and carry them out.

Besides general information and instructions concerning the materials there should be information for each unit. This might give advice on the order in which various activities should be done; how they are to be done (individually, in pairs, in groups), and what medium they should be done in, (for example, 'orally first, then in writing'); how much time they might take; whether they should be done over a short time interval, or paced over a number of days and so on.

The absence of such instructions by no means disqualifies a set of materials for use in self-instruction. At worst, such information can be given by a tutor when it is required; or better, the tutors can provide it for the materials most in use. The idea of undertaking such a task for a whole library of materials is daunting, but if the task is phased over a year or two, and most importantly, if the tutors always write down and save the advice they give to students on such matters, then it can be typed up later and perhaps incorporated in a folder with the materials, or attached in some other way.

An essential accompaniment to instructions is a set of worked examples, and if the examples are clear and well chosen, they may greatly reduce the need for complicated instructions. Often, materials writers use only the first one or two items in an exercise for examples, but these are usually relatively simple, the more difficult ones appearing later. An adequate set of examples would include one or two of the more complex items. The acid test is, of course, whether the examples provide sufficient information for the learner to get on with the exercise.

Language learning advice

In addition to learning instructions, a learner working in a self-instructional mode needs advice about how to go about the job of language learning. She needs advice on such matters as how to do exercises and activities; how to learn vocabulary; whether or not to set out to learn lists of irregular verbs and explicit grammatical rules; how and when to use reference materials such as dictionaries and grammar books; how to plan her work; how to pace it; how intensively to study; how to motivate herself to do it; how to undertake particular tasks like, for example, reading a newspaper article, or listening to a recording to get the gist of the content; how to make use of speakers of the target language; how to assess her attainment; how to keep records of progress; and so on. In other words all learners should, ideally, be made aware of the knowledge good learners have about language learning. This important issue is further discussed in Chapter 7.

This kind of detailed advice could only be expected from courses written specifically for autonomous study, but apparently, even those are rather limited in the advice they give (Chaix and O'Neil 1978). Also, the advice to learners in many of the areas above will differ according to the preferred language teaching/learning method of the materials writer, so there could be some diversity of view between the textbook writer and a tutor advising a learner. However, the more likely situation is that no advice will be given, and so the tutor has the choice of:

- supplying advice as part of the preparation before learners begin on the language learning task, or better, during the initial language learning period; *or*
- preparing a booklet for learners which would include this advice together, maybe, with other things such as, for example, a needs analysis questionnaire, personal contract forms and some kind of record keeping system.

Feedback and tests

The provision of feedback to the learners in the form of answers and explanations to exercises provides a major opportunity for learning in self-instructional materials. A number of published courses now provide answer keys in students' books, and claim thereby that the course is suitable for self-instruction. However, learners need more than simply the correct answer. They need to know *why* they are wrong, *where* they went wrong, and sometimes they need to know how they got the correct answer. Among the techniques for giving feedback, the simplest is to provide a comprehensive and clear description of the language point as part of the learning materials. If the learner then gets wrong answers, she can refer to this description to see why they were wrong. This is only suitable for exercises on discrete aspects of language, however. Alternative techniques suitable for both discrete language items and more global activities are those which predict the learners' answers and provide commentary on the basis of the predictions. The easiest way to do this is to use a multiple choice questioning technique. The materials writer predicts two or three incorrect answers, preferably on the basis of responses from previous learners, and gives explanations in the answer key of why they were wrong. The writer can also give an explanation of why the correct response is right. This helps learners who may have arrived at the correct response for the wrong reasons, and it may help those who got it right validly to articulate the learning point. Some listening and speaking production activities may not be amenable to a multiple choice format. The easiest way of getting feedback on these, and one which learners require as a fallback position anyway, is to get the opinion of a competent user of the language.

Self-instructional materials must provide learners with ways of assessing their achievement at regular intervals, and preferably with suggestions about desirable remedial work. The whole matter of self-assessment is the subject of Chapter 8, so here I will restrict myself to discussing criteria for evaluating the tests. The absence of tests in course materials is a serious drawback, but need not disqualify the course from use for self-instruction since it is always possible for the tutors to prepare tests themselves. Once again, however, this is not a decision to be taken lightly, since the preparation of tests could amount to a lot of work. But if the course is otherwise suitable, you may feel that the work is justified. A partial alternative is to train learners in self-instructional techniques.

Where tests do exist, we must be concerned about their adequacy. This can be estimated from the following factors:

- *The validity of the tests.* How far do they actually test what they claim to? For example, if the tests in a course aiming to teach spoken communicative language consisted mainly of items about grammatical rules, one might have doubts about their validity.
- *The coverage of the tests*: Do they make a reasonable sample of the material in the relevant units?
- *The level of the tests.* Are the tests appropriate to the level of the target learners, and thereby to the objectives of the materials?

Record keeping

It is very important for autonomous learners to feel that they are making progress in the task, and a useful psychological aid to this is keeping records. These can be records of scores for exercises and tests, expressed numerically or in graph form, and they can include records of language items covered so far. (See Appendix D(I) and Carver and Dickinson 1981 for some suggestions.) Once again, the lack of a record keeping system in the materials can easily be made good by the tutors concerned with the self-instruction programme.

Reference materials

Although many learners will have grammar books and reference materials available, their most convenient reference source will be the learning materials themselves. The information presented should be limited to that which is relevant to the stated objectives and written in a way which is intelligible to learners. It should make references to the occurrences of the items in the text, so contextualising them. It should also make cross-references to other units in which the items are dealt with. Most importantly, we can expect the materials to give information on *functions*, *notions*, and *discourse*, which learners would be less likely to find in grammars. The explanations may be in the mother tongue for those at the lower levels of language learning, but post-intermediate learners may be able to cope with target language explanations, in which case they are valuable examples of the authentic use of the language. Whatever language they are in, they must be simple and clear, and diagrams and illustrations may be helpful. References to the occurrences of the item in the text of the materials may also help learners to understand the explanations, and this also helps them to work out meaning in the text.

In addition to references to the relevant items, cross-references to related explanations in other units are very useful.

Reference materials in *vocabulary* may be presented as a single glossary, and/or separate lists may be supplied in each unit of the materials. A single glossary (a recapitulative list) is a very useful reference facility for learners, helping them to recover meanings for words they have learnt but subsequently forgotten. Word lists in each unit are less important as a reference, but they are useful as an *aide-mémoire* of what vocabulary has been covered.

If word lists are to be used for reference purposes then clearly they must supply the meaning of the word in some way. The most appropriate way of doing this will, once again, differ with the level of the target learner; beginners require either a translation into the mother tongue, or visual clues, whilst more advanced learners may be able to cope with definitions in the target language. It is important that word meaning is related to the context of the occurrence of the word, and so the glossary should make reference to key occurrences.

There are particular difficulties about producing reference materials for the *spoken language*. Learners will wish to find out how to pronounce individual words, what particular intonation contours actually sound like, and what they mean in particular contexts, what the effects are of elisions in the production of utterances and so on. The use only of written notations for these is not enough and the only satisfactory system is a combination of cassette recording and notation. In addition, instructions on learning pronunciation would be valuable for the self-instructing learner. This might consist of a brief and simple introduction to concepts such as *phoneme* and *syllable*, *intonation* and *rhythm*, and their effects on meaning and discourse.

Indexing

A good index (or contents list) is essential in a course book to be used for self-instruction, to enable the learners to find explanations of grammatical or discourse points. The index, however, also extends the use of the book into a source of material on specific, discrete learning points, and so makes it more useful as a self-access resource.

Motivational factors

There are several factors which may help to motivate the learner to use the materials, and therefore contribute towards the maintenance of general motivation to learn the target language. The most obvious of these is the attractiveness of the book, the layout, type face, colour work, illustrations and so on. These are matters which are also very important in materials produced within an institution. Such materials should be as professional looking as possible, and contain, where possible, such things as illustrations and colour work. These requirements are likely to be very difficult to meet for many institutions, but it is always possible to produce the materials with a reasonable type face, cleanly duplicated, and to avoid having great blocks of type on the page. Other motivational factors include *accessibility*, which refers to how easy it is to understand how to use the materials, how well organised they are to make for ease of use and so on The *size of unit* is also an important consideration. The learning load for the 'average' learner should be relatively small per unit, so that learners do not have to make a big investment of time and effort to complete one unit. Good self-instructional materials will not only state objectives clearly, but will also *explain objectives*; that is they will explain why it is important to achieve particular objectives in a particular order, and perhaps in combination with other objectives. Finally, some course books include encouragement and warnings to the learner – for example, 'Never get discouraged', or 'Do not be impatient. You are not merely marking time, but making progress, slowly but surely' (Chaix and O'Neil, 1978:47). Some learners find these motivating.

Progression

One of the major factors influencing motivation among language learners is that of progression. Students working in a self-access resource centre who are wallowing around doing a bit of this and a bit of that, with no very clear idea of where they are progressing to, very quickly get demoralised and dissatisfied. Clearly one requirement is to find some way of mapping out a set of objectives for learners, and one way suggested in this book is through Needs Identification and Personal Contracts (see Chapter 5).

A second aspect of progression is concerned with advising the learner how to continue work on a particular set of objectives – for example, advice to study a given structural point in a written text having studied it in a spoken text; or suggestions about what a learner might go on to, having satisfied herself that a particular objective has been achieved. Conventional course books control this kind of progression by assuming that the learner is going to work through the lessons from beginning to end. McCafferty (ND) controls it through the Pathways suggestions in his Networks, and the Circle Model (see Chapter 3) achieves it through offering a limited set of options and allowing learners to choose among these. Whatever the system, it is useful for each unit of material to indicate parallel units and units on the next level.

Another aspect of progression is concerned with advising the learner to look out for appropriate opportunities to use the target language in authentic contexts. This includes reading newspapers and books, watching TV, listening to the radio and to recordings, and speaking the language.

4.4 Conclusion

Materials for self-instruction obviously need to be different in some respects from materials designed to be used with a teacher. This chapter has been concerned with identifying these differences, and with suggesting ways that suitable materials can be produced. One aspect of such materials is the support they give to the learners in their learning. The following chapter is also concerned with supporting learners, though in rather different ways.

5 Supporting the learner in self-instruction

In our brief examination of the teacher's role in the introduction to Part II we saw that the teacher was involved with the student's learning in several ways other than teaching. The teacher is often involved in pedagogical planning; that is, determining aims and objectives, and selecting materials. He has several managerial and organisational responsibilities, such as determining a programme of work, deciding on the materials to be used within the programme, deciding on the pace of work, and where it will be done, and so on. In addition the teacher has an important role in counselling and supporting the learner.

The question we are asking throughout this book is how far the learner can take back these and other responsibilities from the teacher and how the learner might be assisted in this. In addition many learners who are exploring the possibilities of self-instruction are doing so because they have language learning requirements for which they cannot find provision in institutions. In such cases there is an acute practical need to supply these learners with help in taking responsibility for their own learning, since no alternatives to self-instruction are available.

The learner's requirements are listed in the form of a flow chart in figure 20 and each is examined in more detail within the chapter. Ways of providing the appropriate assistance for an autonomous learner are then suggested. I need to emphasise once again that I am not advocating autonomy for everyone; I am simply exploring the most extreme case, recognising that in any teaching/learning situation there is likely to be a compromise between teaching and self-instruction. I join McCafferty in believing that the ideal system is one which allows the learner to take as much responsibility for his own learning as he wishes to, and which makes provision both for those who want full autonomy and those who do not want any!

5.1 The analysis of learners' needs

If we mean by 'needs' specific requirements that learners have for the foreign language they are studying, then the vast majority of learners do not have any. They are deemed to require what the syllabus offers them, and the syllabus is likely to be closely related to the examination (which

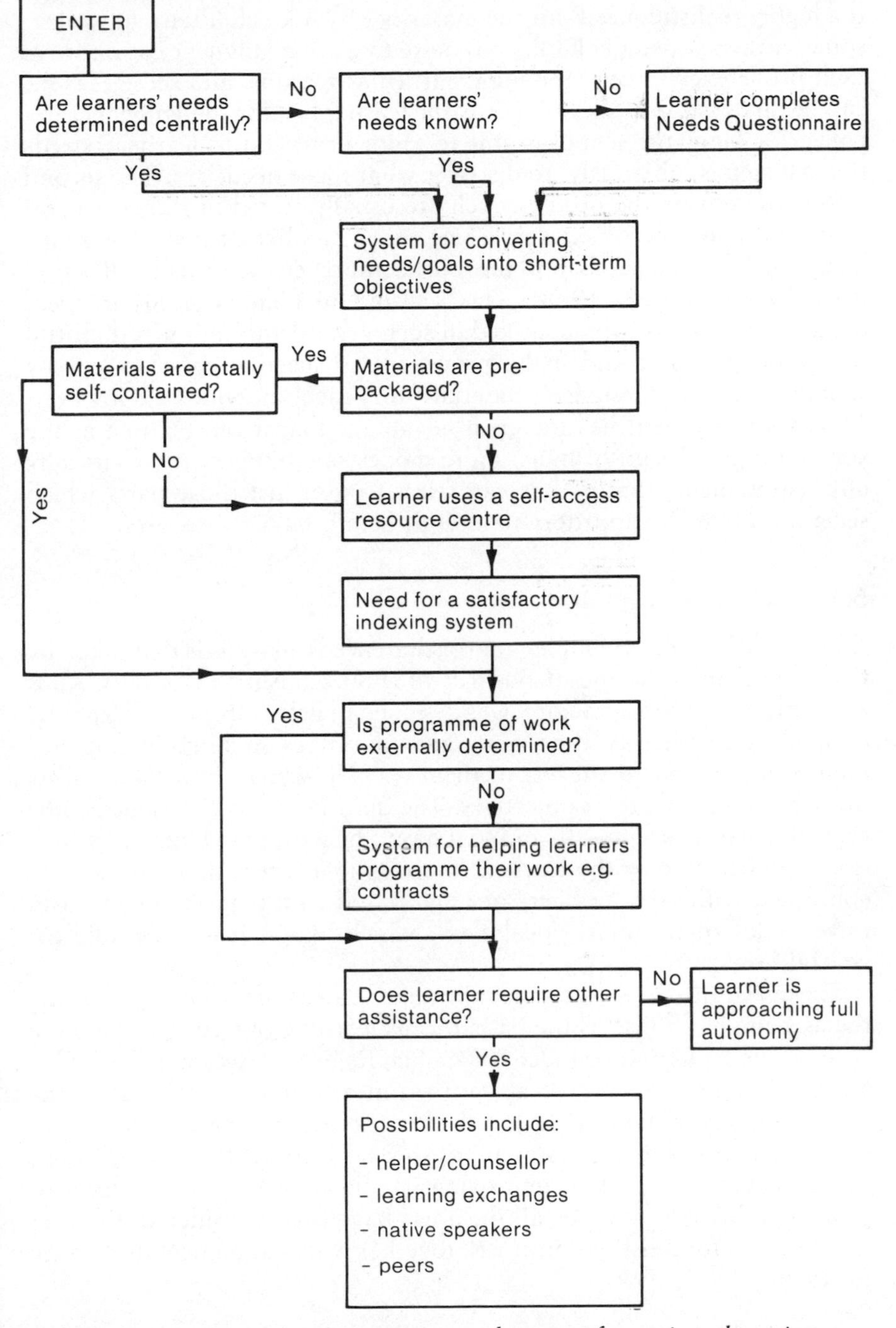

Figure 20 *Learners' requirements and ways of meeting them in self-instruction*

is a highly realistic 'need' for the majority of school children). However, some learners – usually adults – require to learn a language, or improve their proficiency in one, for some particular reasons, and these reasons can be analysed into specific needs the learner has for the language. If a college or language school is able to tailor provision to learners' needs the first step is, obviously, to discover what those needs are. The second step is to convert the needs, which are usually stated in rather general terms, into specific objectives. There are a number of instruments for analysing learners' needs, and the most comprehensive of them all is that designed by Munby (1978). This sets out to identify needs in great detail. Indeed needs are identified in such great detail that it is doubtful if any institution could make provision for meeting them except by writing specially designed materials for each individual. However, Munby's instrument has the great advantage that it can be used as the source for the design of much more modest instruments to fit virtually any requirement; that is, one can select from it just those parts which seem useful, at the appropriate level of detail.

5.1.1 Cousin

A rather different and simpler approach to needs analysis is that taken by Cousin and his colleagues (Cousin *et al.* 1980, Cousin 1982a). His 'Aims and Objectives Questionnaire' was designed to help self-directed learners of English to identify their aims and objectives in English language improvement, and to suggest to them ways in which they could assess the achievement of their objectives. The questionnaire is designed to be used by the learner himself, and so it has to be written in language which is comprehensible to the learner. In fact, the learners that Cousin was concerned with were teachers of English and so the questionnaire uses rather a lot of technical vocabulary, which makes it less suitable for general users.

The questionnaire suggests a wide range of areas of the language which the user might choose as the basis for his learning objectives. These are such things as 'Correct Model' (of spoken English), 'Accent and Dialect' and 'Reading Speed'. These are printed in a column on the left of the questionnaire, and the user is asked to decide on (and to record in subsequent columns) his estimate of the necessity of the area for him, the importance to him of improving it, and then to give it a level of priority in his work. When all the areas have been considered, the user has the basis for a list of objectives, together with a statement of priority for each.

5.1.2 Allwright

Allwright (1982) attempts to design a system of needs analysis which starts with the learners' perceptions of their needs in their own terms. Allwright carefully distinguishes between *needs, wants* and *lacks*. Needs are those skills which a learner perceives as being relevant to him; wants are a subset of needs, those which a learner puts at a high priority given the time available; and a lack is the difference a learner perceives between his present competence in a particular skill and the competence he wishes to achieve.

Allwright is concerned both with helping learners to identify skill areas and with identifying their preferred ways (strategies) of achieving those skills, and the core of the system consists of two questionnaires – one relevant to each. The first is concerned with the identification of needs, wants and lacks as defined above. As is shown in figure 21, the learners write in their own list of needs using their own descriptions. The learners' wants can be discerned from the first two columns labelled *Frequency* and *Importance*.

In the example, the learner places 'Writing formal letters' about half way down. Though the frequency of use is very low, the learner gives it a high importance rating, which indicates it as a fairly important 'want'. It also gets a high score for 'lack' since the learner requires a very high proficiency but rates his present proficiency as very low. The final column, *Confidence*, asks the learner to record the degree of certainty he has in making these judgements.

People often find it very difficult to decide what language learning or language improvement needs they have. It may be clear enough when you are attempting to take part in a technical discussion in a foreign language that this is an ability which is of some importance to you and at which you are not very good, but three months later when you sit down to fill in a needs questionnaire form you may have forgotten. Allwright assists his students by suggesting that they first work together in a workshop group to generate ideas on what the members of the group need English for now, what they needed it for in the past, and what they anticipate they will need English for in the future. Each workshop group is provided with a discussion guide which asks the individual to consider the answers to three questions:

– What *do* you need English for?
– What *have* you needed English for?
– What do you *expect* to need English for in the future?

Each individual then shares his answers with the rest of the group, and a group response is drawn up. The members of the group then use this list individually as an *aide-mémoire* in completing the Needs Questionnaire.

NEEDS

++ very high
+ high
O medium
- low
-- very low

Name ....Wisniewski........
Date ....3 – 09 – 1979........

NEEDS	FREQUENCY	IMPORTANCE	PROFICIENCY REQUIRED	PROFICIENCY NOW	CONFIDENCE
reading for pleasure	++	++	O	O	+
reading newspapers, listening to radio (for information)	++	++	O	O	+
survival English (being abroad as a tourist)	–	++	–	+	+
social conversation	–	+	++	–	O
writing private letters	– –	O	O	–	+
writing formal letters	– –	+	++	– –	–
giving a lecture	– –	++	+	– –	O
listening to a lecture	O	O	+	O	+
taking part in a scientific discussion	– –	O	+	–	O
writing scientific papers	– –	++	++	–	+
reading scientific (professional) books and journals	++	++	+	–	O
speed reading	– –	–	++	– –	–

Figure 21 Allwright: Needs Questionnaire

The next stage is for the learners to think about and record their preferences about ways of studying English in order to achieve their needs. A similar procedure is followed with individuals and groups using a second guide to draw up a list of activities, strategies and techniques they use for learning or improving English.

Allwright's guide distinguishes among activities which might be used in class from those a learner may use in private or he may use while interacting with speakers of English. Individuals then select from this list those strategies etc. which they use for learning or improving English. Against each activity the individual records his personal preference rating, the frequency of use that strategy is put to, its usefulness and how efficient the learner is at using it (see figure 22).

This information can then be used by a counsellor to help individual learners to decide on their wants and lacks in terms of learning strategies. In the example given by Allwright, reproduced here, the learner rates 'improving pronunciation by conversation with the teacher' (second from top) as high in preference and very high in usefulness, yet he uses it rarely and regards himself as only moderately efficient at using it. It seems likely then that this learner would appreciate further practice in using this strategy, and advice on how to use it more efficiently.

It is, of course, not possible for a counsellor to be totally confident in interpreting these completed questionnaires, and so the third stage in this procedure is an interview with each learner to discuss both their needs and preferred strategies and to draw up a provisional programme of work. In the circumstances in which Allwright used this scheme, a provisional timetable was suggested which offered three modes of learning: class work, self-access study, and writing workshops. The interviews in this context would be concerned with helping each learner to decide on the best ways to meet his needs within this framework, and simultaneously for the counsellors to confirm their interpretations of the questionnaires.

»»→

LANGUAGE LEARNING STRATEGIES – PERSONAL PROFILE

NAME ..KRAKOWSKI..........

DATE ..5th September 1978..

HH - very high
H - high
M - medium
L - low
LL - very low
} Columns 3, 4, 5, 6

1 CATEGORY	2 LEARNING ACTIVITY/ STRATEGY	3 PERSONAL PREFERENCE RATING	4 FREQUENCY OF PERSONAL USE	5 PERSONAL USEFULNESS RATING	6 'OWN EFFICIENCY AT USING IT' RATING
In class	Learning words and language rules	M	M	M	M
	doing exercises	M	L	M	M
	answering the questions	H	L	H	H
	improving the pronunciation by conversation with teacher	H	LL	HH	M
	writing the dictations	M	L	M	L
Privately	reading papers and books	M	HH	M	M
	conversation with a friend who knows English better	HH	M	H	H
	talking with guests from abroad	M	M	M	M
	translating texts from Polish to English	H	M	M	M
In real-life encounters	asking, answering and talking with people during staying abroad	H	LL	H	H

Figure 22 Allwright: Language Learning Strategies

5.1.3 Harding-Esch

Harding-Esch (1982) takes a rather simpler approach to needs analysis, and suggests a system which, if necessary, can be used entirely by the learner himself without help from a counsellor. When potential users first come to the self-access language learning facility in the University of Cambridge (see Chapter 3 for a description of the system), they are directed to a folder called the 'Square One Kit'. This contains all the information necessary to use the facilities efficiently, and includes a leaflet on needs analysis (see figure 23).

The preliminary purpose of the leaflet is to show users that they need to think carefully about their intentions and purposes in learning a language before selecting materials and getting involved in what might turn out to be unsuitable work. An additional use of the leaflet is to act as a basis for consultation with a counsellor. Once the user has thought through the questions in this leaflet, and decided on preliminary answers, the counsellor can use the responses as a basis first for discussion and then for advising on materials and activities. Harding-Esch gives an example of a completed questionnaire from a learner of Turkish (see figure 24).

→

Motivation	What is your attitude towards the community whose language you want to learn? How much does it matter if you don't succeed? Do you need to learn the language to be able to achieve certain specific tasks or do you want to learn enough to be accepted as a member of the foreign community?
Aims	What do you want to be able to do in the language? Do you want to communicate in the written or the spoken language? or both? Will it be enough if you just understand the language (at least in the first instance)? For you, is it sufficient to learn just enough language for communication to occur?
Functions	What use will you be making of the language? What kind of situations will you have to perform in? (telephone? lectures? seminars? shops? etc.) What functions of language will you primarily need? (explaining, persuading, seeking information, contradicting, etc.) What will your relationship be with the people you will be dealing with? (friends, inferiors, superiors, etc.)
Information	What kind of linguistic information do you need to meet your needs? Which are the most important: technical vocabulary? the precise meaning of intonation? correct pronunciation? a set of ready-made sentences to get by with?
Activities	What need you do to learn what you want? How much time can you devote to it? What are your learning habits? Do you like working on your own? Is the Language Lab suitable? Do you need help? (Dictionary, radio, newspapers, grammars, contact with native speakers, etc.) Do you know native speakers who would agree to talk with you in their own language? Do you make full use of other possibilities, e.g., the radio? sub-titled film? etc.

Figure 23 University of Cambridge Needs Analysis

Case 4: **English native speaker; 3rd year Engineering student; had a 2 year contract in Turkey starting the following year; beginning Turkish from scratch.**

 otivation	Extremely high; success essential.
A ims	Surviving in Turkey: shopping, finding lodgings, etc., social life; discussing efficiently with Turkish engineers (although he knew most would speak English); understanding the workers in his department and dealing with them without too much difficulty.
 unctions	Asking about the language; apologizing for not understanding; asking people to correct his Turkish; asking for information; explaining; giving advice; giving orders; suggesting; use of these functions with colleagues, seniors and people working under him.
I nformation	Correct pronunciation (must be understood); survival kit of sentences for everyday life in the first instances; as much comprehension as possible; technical vocabulary (decided he would learn it very rapidly once in Turkey).
 ctivities	Spent 1 hour 3 times a week in the Lab, using the Turkish basic course; used Lab's list of Turkish speakers in Cambridge; exchanged language lessons with Turkish student weekly; saw Turkish lector for list of books about Turkey and discussed them with Turkish student; began listening to BBC South European Service after about a term, listening to the news and commentary just after having heard it in English.

Figure 24

5.1.4 Designing a needs questionnaire

On the basis of these examples we can list a series of considerations for the designer of a needs questionnaire.

- Is the questionnaire to be used by the learner or by a specialist (teacher, helper or counsellor)? This affects the terminology used in the questions and the degree of detail the questionnaire sets out to elicit.
- Is the questionnaire complete in itself, or is it designed to act as the basis for an interview with a specialist?
- Is it designed to elicit needs irrespective of whether facilities exist for meeting them or only to the level for which teaching/learning facilities and materials exist?
- Should it elicit information on learners' preferred learning strategies etc.?
- Will the questionnaire be concerned with identifying the time available; that is, the total time to the date by which the target language must be learned (for example, the point of departure to undertake field studies or the date of a conference in the foreign country etc.; or simply the time available each week for language study)?
- Should the questionnaire endeavour to analyse needs into short-term objectives?
- Will the questionnaire attempt to suggest appropriate materials to meet objectives?
- Will the questionnaire attempt to guide the learner in ways of assessing the achievement of objectives?

5.2 Learner contracts

One of the main differences between learning in an autonomous mode and learning in a teacher-led class is the means through which the learning is structured. All language learners need to feel that their learning is purposeful to be successful. Purposefulness is, at least in part, dependent on the structuring of the learning. The identification of relevant objectives, their incorporation into a realistic learning programme, the decision on what materials to use, over what period, and with what intensity, and a clear idea of how the learning is to be assessed, are all of crucial importance in efficient learning. The teacher in a conventional class structures the learners' work; the autonomous learner must provide the necessary structure for himself. Learners who have no clear idea of their objectives, who are wandering from one piece of material to another with no definite idea of where they are progressing, or what they want to achieve, very quickly get dispirited and are likely to give up their attempts at language learning.

One way of providing structure in a self-instructional learning mode is the learner contract. A contract provides a learner with a framework for his planning, and a brief check-list of things he has to take into account. The minimal contract will suggest to the learner that he decides merely *what work* he is going to do over *what period*. The contract which is illustrated below suggests that the learner makes rather more decisions. It asks him to decide not only what work he is going to do, but what activities he is going to engage in, what resources he is going to use, and how he is going to demonstrate that he has met the objectives he set himself. It needs to be said straight away that completing a contract form of this kind is a difficult task and involves the learner in considerable thought. When learners first come across contract learning it is essential that they are given careful preparation for completing the contract form. This is discussed briefly at the end of this section and more fully in Appendix A.

A learner contract is an agreement between the learner and the tutor, or between the learner and himself. Since its purpose is to help the learner to give structure to his work, it is essential it is taken seriously by both the learner and the tutor, and that the learner recognises it as binding. Contracts should be binding, but not rigidly so; it would be foolish to expect a learner to be bound to a contract he subsequently recognises as ill-designed. On the other hand, it would negate the point of having a contract if the learner did not feel that it was normally binding.

The contract form illustrated in figure 25 is one which we used in SCEO and which was adapted from Knowles (1975). It has been completed to show what a learner at an advanced level might contract to do over a month. Advanced learners can complete the form in English, but less proficient learners may need to use their mother tongue, and indeed the form itself would need to be translated into the mother tongue.

The form is divided into seven columns and the headings in the first four function as a brief check-list to remind the learner of the decisions he needs to take in planning his own work. The first column asks the learner to decide on what learning objectives he is going to tackle. The response in the illustration gives, first, the general learning area (for example, Reading speed in Entry 1), and then makes a more detailed specification of objectives where this is easily possible. Thus, the objective Reading speed is further specified as 'improve speed from 100 words per minute (wpm) to 120 wpm without reducing comprehension.' Entry 3 in the same column, however, does not make a very detailed specification – for the very good reason that it is difficult even for language

LANGUAGE SKILLS CONTRACT

NAME: Djibril GROUP: Advanced DATE: 1 October

Skill area for improvement – learning objectives	Proposed activities – what you are going to do	Proposed resources – what you are going to use	Target date for completion	Ways of demonstrating achievement – how you are going to test yourself	Tutor's initials	Date completed
1. Reading speed Improve speed from 100 w.p.m. to 120 w.p.m. without reducing comprehension	Timed reading of prepared passages	Reading speed builders Box IV; Level – blue	1 Nov	– Use test items in the card for comprehension and get >80% – Reach >120 w.p.m. on five consecutive cards		
2. Seminar discussion skills – Break into a discussion – Disagree politely with another speaker – State an alternative viewpoint	– Take part in oral skills option → – Try to arrange additional discussions with friends → – Practise during tutorials and seminars in other subjects →	– Supplied by tutor – Try to get a native speaker to take part; watch TV news and discuss current issues; use newspapers – Supplied by tutor	1 Nov	– Judge reactions of other participants – do they look startled/irritated when I join in? – Do I convey my viewpoint? Do I manage to persuade people? Try to get native speaker to monitor my performance		
3. Essay writing – Improve my planning of essays → – Writing essays →	– Plan essays on many topics → – Write one essay per week on one of the topics above →	– Wallace Study Skills in English – Form self-help group from friends (tutor will help with this)	1 Nov	– Use guide in book – Self-assessment schedule – Ask tutor – Ask tutor – Self-assessment – Assessment by self-help group – Tutor to check some essays } Using criteria supplied by tutor		

Figure 25

teachers to specify detailed objectives for essay writing. (It is possible – see Appendix D(II).)

The second and third columns are concerned with what the learner is going to do, and the resources he is going to use. The second column, then, asks the learner to say what he is actually going to do to achieve his objective, whilst the third asks him to specify the materials and other resources he is going to use. The resources he chooses may be materials, such as books or recordings, but they may also include other people. The fourth column 'Target date for completion' is self-explanatory in its meaning but not in its importance. Contracts should be made to cover relatively short time spans for all learners, but especially for less advanced learners. It is important that learners get a sense of achievement at regular intervals, and this is more likely if the period covered by the contract is brief. Moreover, as learners progress through contracts, they gain in sophistication in identifying and specifying objectives; a brief contract period makes it easier to change inappropriate contracts.

Column 5 concerns assessment and asks the learners how they are going to demonstrate that they have achieved their objectives. Most learners find this very difficult to specify, partly because most have little or no experience in doing it, and partly because it is difficult anyway for many objectives. Where the materials being used have been properly designed for self-instruction, or adapted for this learning mode, then there will be self-assessment devices built into them, and so this column will be easy to fill in. However, where learners are using other materials, and authentic texts, then they will usually need a lot of help from the teacher with assessment – at the early stages of self-instruction anyway. (Readers might find Chapter 8 and the associated appendix helpful.) The next column, Tutor's initials, is optional. The requirement that the tutor initials the contract acts as a form of extrinsic motivation to the learner to complete the work. Many learners who are new to self-instruction, and especially those who are used to a system in which the teacher is highly directive, like having the form initialled by the tutor since it gives them a feeling of security. Nevertheless, it is important that learners are weaned away from this need as soon as possible and that they come to recognise their own responsibility for their work. The final column, 'Date completed', acts as a check for the learner of the accuracy of the estimated time, and on the intensity of the work carried out.

The whole notion of contract learning is likely to seem very strange to learners who have not experienced it before. Actually completing a contract form is a difficult task, and learners need practice in it; consequently, it is best introduced gradually. For example, at the beginning, learners may be invited to use a simple contract form to specify what extensive reading each person will cover in the next week. Practice in identifying needs can be combined with the preparation in completing contracts; the teacher's correction of both written and spoken performance gives indications of some of the errors being produced; peer- and self-monitoring may indicate other errors. These can be noted by the learner in a record of progress, and specified as objectives in a simple contract. At this early stage the teacher would need to help with the whole process, and particularly with deciding how the work should be done, what materials to use and how to assess achievement. The learners' practice in contract completion is restricted to identifying needs/objectives.

The next stage in preparation is to help learners to complete a full contract form. One way of doing this is to divide the class into small groups of three and provide each group with a sample contract and a set of questions against which the groups evaluate the contract. Following a class discussion of the evaluation, each individual completes a contract and then other members of the group of three comment on it using the evaluation questions. A full description of this process is given in Appendix A.

The contract system has several attributes which are important in self-instruction. Primarily, it is a means of breaking free of a lockstep system in that it acts as a framework to enable the learner to structure his work, either individually or together with others in a group. This structuring includes determining goals, determining deadlines for completing work, and determining the intensity of work. It also includes specifying the means of evaluating how well the goals have been achieved. Thus, it helps the learner to develop autonomy from the teacher and from the control of a single textbook. For those learners who have no ambitions towards autonomy, or who are in an early stage of preparation for it, the contract system helps them to learn about objectives and assessment, and therefore to develop a greater awareness of language and the process of language learning.

5.3 Other ways of supporting learners

All of the ways of supporting learners discussed in this part concern people. As I have tried to make clear throughout this book, the teacher has a vital role to play in supporting learners in a self-instructional mode (that is until the learners become autonomous). Also, the learners themselves are very important in providing support to one another through self-help groups and 'study buddy' arrangements. Furthermore, it may be possible to fix up learning exchanges, in which, for example, a speaker of English who is learning French works with a speaker of French who is learning English. Finally, native (or competent) speakers of the target language can provide very valuable help in supplying language input, talking with the learner and, maybe, assisting the learner in self-assessment.

5.3.1 Support through groups

A statement frequently heard in connection with self-instruction is that self-instruction does not entail isolation. There is no reason for the self-instructing learner to work in isolation; equally, there is no compulsion to work in a group. For most learners, however, being a member of a group of peers who are all striving towards similar ends, and who are struggling with similar difficulties and problems, can be a tremendous help in maintaining morale, and in motivation.

Our experience with self-directed learning in the Scottish Centre for Education Overseas demonstrates unequivocally that most learners prefer to be members of an identifiable group, and also that they prefer to have a particular tutor with specific responsibility towards that group. This does not mean that all the members of the group need to be working on the same language skills at the same time, nor, indeed, at the same level. It does mean though, that the group functions as a group for activities such as seminars on needs analysis, completing personal learning contracts, and for 'learner training' – activities designed to teach learners how to use authentic materials, how to assess themselves and so on (see Chapter 7.) In addition, this group also constitutes the first source for forming sub-groups for such things as essay writing, and for oral interaction activities.

Conversely there are some learning situations in which it is not easy to form groups. Where learners are able to attend the institution only rarely – perhaps once a month – to consult a helper, it is not easy to organise a group. One simpler alternative is the 'study buddy' arrangement, where one learner is introduced to another working on similar objectives at a similar level. This arrangement gives each learner the support of at least one other, ensures that learners have someone to sympathise with them in their difficulties, gives each person someone else with whom they can discuss problems and to turn to for advice, and with whom they can work out mutual problems. Finally it provides for each learner another individual with whom they can carry out interaction tasks and with whom they can practise using the language.

A fellow learner, of course, is not the best source for new language input; also, though a fellow learner may be the most satisfactory person with whom to try out new language initially, learners also want to use the language with native or competent speakers. A number of systems that were described in Chapter 3 make arrangements to introduce learners to native speakers of the target language. The Cambridge Sound and Video Library maintains a catalogue of speakers of various languages, drawn mainly from the postgraduate students at the university. Language learners wishing to make contact with a native speaker of their target language can do so through the counsellor associated with the library (Harding and Tealby 1981:104). In the Assisted Self Tutoring scheme (AST) at Aston University, contact with a native speaker informant is a built-in part of the system: '... the speaker goes to the informant in order to obtain specific information, whether it be pronunciation, a statement concerning syntax or semantics, or confirmation of the correctness of exercises or a previously learnt term' (Ager, Clavering and Galleymore 1980:21). Everyone writing about the use of informants in a self-instructional system is at pains to stress that informants are not teachers and that this should be made totally clear to both the informant and the learner. The ideological desire towards self-instruction usually plays little part in this; the problem is that, often, informants are rather poor teachers!

Other writers, however, recommend using native speakers for teaching purposes, but in the special context of learning exchanges. A learning exchange in language learning is where a native speaker of English for example, wishing to improve his knowledge of French, works with a native speaker of French wishing to improve his knowledge of English. Such schemes are more likely to be successful if the learners are provided with suggestions of activities or even an actual package of work. Dalwood (1977) reports a variety of learning exchange which she describes as a 'Reciprocal Language Learning Course'. In this, groups of French learners of English travelled to Britain and worked for two or three weeks with groups of English learners of French. The level of the groups was around English General Certificate of Education Advanced Level, (that is the level often required for university entrance). Dalwood provided a firm programme of activities, part of which included work in pairs on supplied packages of material. Material was supplied in both French and English and the members of each pair took it in turns to be teacher and taught.

Harding and Tealby (1981:104) also describe the use of learning exchanges at Cambridge. Once the pairs were established, the counsellor made suggestions about possible tasks and activities they might undertake. They comment that the scheme was relatively successful, particularly with undergraduate learners.

5.4 Conclusion

This chapter began by recognising that learners undertaking self-instruction needed, at least initially, much of the support usually provided by the teacher. It suggested ways that such support could be given through needs analysis, through contracts and through peers. Chapter 6, also, is concerned with supporting learners, but more indirectly, through the provision of the means to enable them to carry out their work in a self-access resource centre.

6 Self-access resources

We have already seen that self-instruction may take many forms, and one of these is where the learner, for part or the whole of her learning time, seeks and uses materials from a resource to help achieve her personal objectives. In order to cater for such a learning mode, the appropriate materials have to be available and easily accessible to the learner. This chapter is concerned with one way in which materials can be made accessible to learners. It begins by reviewing the functions of a self-access resource facility, and then examines aspects of the physical organisation of a resource, including a listing of desirable equipment and a discussion of classification and indexing of materials. This is followed by a section on operating the resource, including the preparation of learners to use it.

6.1 Functions of a self-access resource

Self-access means that the learner *can* do the following things, though she may not *have* to do them:

- Decide on what to do; this may include decisions on what objectives to work on, what particular skill area to work on and so on.
- Find the appropriate material to work on for the objectives decided on, or do further practice on something that was begun in class.
- Use the material; this includes such matters as knowing how to do particular activities, what to do first, and next, as well as how to assess yourself on the achievement of the objectives.

All of these have to be possible without help from a tutor; this does not mean that a tutor will never be available, but the whole point of a self-access resource centre is that learners can work on a variety of different tasks without direct supervision.

McCafferty (1982) and Harding-Esch (1982) view the self-access resource as the central facility in the provision made for learning. Learners select this approach to learning either because there are no alternatives (Harding-Esch) or because they positively choose self-instruction (McCafferty). In contrast, self-access learning is used by many other institutions as an addition to the normal classroom provision of a course. Brown (1980:17) says that in her institution the self-access provision caters for students working individually to answer three needs:

- *Remedial*: for students who have gaps in their knowledge or skills, or who are slower than the others in a group.
- *Specific interests*: for students who have specific needs or interests which the rest of the group do not share (for example, agriculture, politics, etc.).
- *Practice in particular skills*: for students who are set a task like interviewing or telephoning, to work on the techniques needed before actually doing the task.

In addition to these functions, Ray Mackay (personal communication) emphasises the importance of the learners regarding the centre as a place where they might simply browse among the materials, have a chat and seek help and encouragement from the staff member on duty. McCafferty (ND:24) summarises all these functions as follows:

- *Access to materials*. This means facilities for such things as perusing, selecting, listening, viewing, sampling, getting copies of print or audio to take away (and these facilities available in minutes rather than hours).
- *Access to activities*. The learner needs people to talk to, to listen to, to discuss, argue and exchange information with, to write to, to practise with, to learn from. It is a function of the centre to bring learners together; to provide a meeting place; initially at least to create the basis and purpose for activities and to provide either monitoring or endorsement of activities.
- *Access to helpers*. This means facilities for making appointments, contacting by telephone, by note, by 'ansaphone'. There is a need for a common language, a record of shared information, progress, problems, a place to meet.

Several writers emphasise the importance of self-access centres being 'user friendly'. Once again McCafferty (ND:8) provides a useful check-list. 'User friendly' means that it has to be easy for the learner to do all the things he needs to do. These include:

- *Access*. Is the building open for long hours? Is it easy to get to the index, to call or find a member of staff?
- *Information*. Is the material fully indexed? Can several people use the index at once? Is the information reasonably comprehensive?
- *Workspace*. Is there a place for learners to look at print and video, listen to and sample tapes, meet in small groups?

– *Availability.* Is it easy for learners to obtain copies of print material and tapes quickly and whenever the centre is open? Is there an effective storage system and an effective reproduction system?
– *Environment.* Is there a place to talk to staff, to leave and collect messages, to arrange activities, to leave work for endorsement?

In both of these lists, McCafferty is, of course, describing the ideal; most teachers operating a centre in a single classroom with little help and inadequate funding have to select which of these facilities to provide.

6.2 Physical organisation

The organisation and layout of a self-access centre will be decided largely in response to what the centre will be used for. So, for example, a self-access centre which concentrates on providing reading materials and reading improvement facilities does not require an area for viewing video recordings. However, a resource centre providing facilities across the whole range of language learning activities requires separate areas for:

– Oral skills: listening and speaking drill type activities
– Listening and viewing
– Reading and writing
– Communicative interaction: playing games, doing role-plays and simulations, and discussion activities
– Consultations with tutors
– The catalogue and other information
– A work and storage area restricted to tutors.

Those materials – print, audio and video – which are on open access would be placed adjacent to the appropriate areas. (See, for some examples, Beswick 1972, Riley and Zoppis 1976.)

Various categories of equipment are either necessary or desirable to carry out these functions. Equipment to provide spoken language input, and to provide facilities for practice in the spoken language includes audio cassette machines and video playback machines.

Dual channel cassette recorders are useful for certain kinds of practice in the spoken language. These are cassette recorders similar to those used in audio active comparative (AAC) language laboratories, which allow the user to record on one channel of the tape while listening to the second (master) channel; subsequently it is possible to listen to both channels together. These are expensive machines costing at least six times the price of a standard cassette recorder, and so only sufficient should be provided for the estimated need for oral skills work. Listening only facilities can be provided very much more cheaply. The cheapest listening facility is a single tape or cassette player with students sitting around it. This can be improved with the addition of a sound distribution box which allows for several headsets to receive the sound from a single source (a tape or cassette recorder, video monitor etc.). Individual listening facilities can be provided at reasonable cost through domestic cassette recorders and headsets. (If the cassette recorders are attached to a table top, this gives a degree of security.)

Video playback facilities are also expensive, especially if individual viewing facilities are envisaged. Costs can be kept down by fitting each video module (video player and monitor) with a sound distribution box. An interesting recent development is interactive video which is essentially a video disc player linked to a micro-computer. The computer controls random access to any part of the video disc so that it is possible, for example, to select video sequences illustrating some particular language point and view them in any order, and repeatedly. It is also possible to incorporate them into a unit of material so that the relevant sequence is presented whenever appropriate for the unit – both in the body of the material and/or as a remedial sequence following an assessment. The major problems with interactive video at the time of writing are the lack of suitable software, and the cost of producing relevant video programmes. However, a system based on a video cassette recorder has recently been reported by Little and Davis (1986). This would make interactive video available at a much reduced cost, and would allow the use of existing video programmes (at the sacrifice of the very fast response of the disc player).

In addition to equipment to provide language input to the learner, it is also highly desirable to have equipment available for recording sound and video, and making and copying instructional materials. Such equipment might include a radio tuner, good quality sound recorder, and a video recorder to make recordings of those radio and television programmes that copyright allows. If the video recorder is also equipped with a camera, this extends the scope of making one's own materials – recording lectures for example, or taking it outdoors and recording aspects of daily life. Similarly, if there is a sound conditioned room available, and appropriate microphones, in-house listening materials can be produced to suit the needs of the learners. A fast copier for audio cassettes is also very useful. This device can copy a master recording on to two cassettes at eight times the normal speed. In addition, a photocopier for copying in-house material saves having to keep a large number of copies of print materials available. Finally, a device which is useful for learning, producing materials and managing resources is the micro-computer. Together with disc drive and printer it can be used in computer-assisted learning, computer-managed learning, and as a word processor and storage system for print documents.

6.3 Classification and indexing systems

The way the materials are organised in the resource to make them accessible to users will have a crucial effect on the success or failure of self-access learning. There are two aspects to this organisation; on the one hand there is the physical position – on shelves, in drawers, and so on – of each item in the resource; and on the other hand there is the record in a catalogue of what items are in the resource and their location.

6.3.1 Classification systems

The way the items are categorised and thereby located in the resource is generally referred to as the classification system. It is usual for self-access resources to use a system in which the items are collected together in sensible categories (rather than, for example, one in which they are stacked simply according to an accession number referring to when they were acquired). Thus, in a language learning resource the items may be shelved according to whether they are related to listening, speaking, reading and writing for example, and then perhaps subdivided within these categories into listening and note taking, literature, dictation and so on.

Classification systems are very limited in the amount of information they can provide easily. Any one item can only be in one place, so a book which is relevant to listening, speaking and reading has to be placed in one of these categories, and if the learner was totally dependent on searching through the shelves and drawers for the materials she wanted then such a book might be missed. It is possible to colour-code items, so providing a second level of classification. Thus, materials suitable for advanced learners might have a red circle stuck on the spine, intermediate might have a green circle, and so on. Nevertheless, classification systems are essentially uni-dimensional. What is required in addition is an *index*. An index is a store of information about the materials, often recorded on cards, which is recorded in such a way as to provide easy retrieval of information on a range of questions; what materials there are for particular skills, by particular authors, on particular topics, and so on. An index is not limited by the physical position of the item on the shelves, and it is multi-dimensional, being able to provide information on as many facets of the materials as seems worthwhile.

Given the limitations on classification systems, it is important to give a lot of thought to the choice of system that is to be adopted, so that it is maximally useful yet as simple as possible for learners to use. Two systems are illustrated, the first from the Bell College, Saffron Walden, and the second from CRAPEL at the University of Nancy II, France.

Bell College

The materials in the study centre are arranged according to a series of modules. There are five in all:

MODULE 1: *Listening*

1.1 Listening only
1.2 Listening and note taking
1.3 Songs
1.4 Dictations
1.5 Technical

MODULE 2: *Speaking*

2.1 Pronunciation
2.2 Paced reading
2.3 Vocabulary
2.4 Drills

MODULE 3: *Books with tapes*

3.1 Course books
3.2 Listening books
3.3 Study skills
3.4 Technical

MODULE 4: *Reading and writing*

4.1 Composition
4.2 Note taking
4.3 Library
4.4 Grammar
4.5 Using reference books
4.6 Readers and cassettes
4.7 Money
4.8 Handwriting
4.9 Shapes

MODULE 5: *Examinations*

5.1 TOEFL

5.2 RSA Communicative Examination
5.3 ARELS
5.4 Cambridge First Certificate
5.5 Cambridge Proficiency

Each item – cassette, folder, book etc., – has printed on it the module number, the category number, and a third number which indicates the number of items of this type and the place of the example in it. Thus, 4.2.7 indicates that the item is in the 'Reading and writing' module, is concerned with note taking, and is the seventh worksheet etc. within note taking. The material is cross-referenced for subject in the catalogue. This system has the vital quality of simplicity of use (though Sheila Brown says that some students have difficulty in remembering three numbers), and it would not be too demanding on teachers putting in new materials.

CRAPEL

A somewhat different scheme has been devised for the Sound and Video Library at the University of Nancy II (Riley and Zoppis 1976:131). This is based on a key word system. Each main entry key word is a general topic label, and the topic can be divided up into sub-topics indefinitely, for example:

LITERATURE

– book review
– drama
– essays
– novel ... etc.

The list of key words is displayed prominently above the catalogue, which contains cards (see figure 26) on each item in the resource, filed according to key words, and according to author/title. The catalogue contains a generous amount of cross-referencing, which reduces the risk of a student missing an item.

Most of the entry labels are self-explanatory:

C: *Code.* This refers to the key word listing mentioned above.
D: *Title* and *Series.* The series name acts as a useful further cross-reference.
E: *Written document.* This refers to any written material accompanying an audio or video recording.
I: *Archive No.* This is of no interest to students, since the Nancy Sound and Video Library is not self-access. The archive number enables the attendant to find the document in the collection.

<table>
<tr><td colspan="2">A : Author, interviewer</td><td>B : Source</td><td>C : Code</td></tr>
<tr><td colspan="3">D : Title :
Series :</td><td>E : Written document</td></tr>
<tr><td colspan="4">F : Synopsis :</td></tr>
<tr><td colspan="4">G : Key words - cross-references</td></tr>
<tr><td>H : Spontaneous
Non-spont</td><td rowspan="2">J : Accents</td><td rowspan="2">K : Speed</td><td>L : Length of recording</td></tr>
<tr><td>I : Archive N°</td><td>M : Date of recording</td></tr>
</table>

Figure 26

6.3.2 Indexing systems

There are basically three choices of indexing systems: a straightforward card catalogue, co-ordinate indexes and micro-computers. It is not possible here to give more than a brief outline of each system, and readers who require more information will need to consult specialist literature. Good sources of information on indexing systems include, for education in general, Beswick (1972, 1975), and for language learning, Blake (1982), Riley and Zoppis (1976) and Windeatt (1981).

The simple card catalogue will be familiar to most readers. It provides the necessary information by dividing up the relevant field of knowledge into several subjects, and listing the relevant materials under each as appropriate. Co-ordinate indexes operate by having some mechanical system to enable the user to sort cards according to a number of criteria simultaneously. For example, suppose a learner wanted a selection of audio recordings about hi-jacking, in an American English accent, which are spontaneous discussions (rather than, for example, a scripted monologue). With a simple card index he would have to make several searches, beginning by searching alphabetically through an index of topics; with a co-ordinate index he would need to make only one. There are two forms of co-ordinate index: edge-punched cards, and the optical coincidence card index (OCCI). (This latter system is well described in Beswick 1972, 1975.) Edge punched cards use index cards which have holes punched all round the perimeter. Each indexing category – topic, learning skill, level and so on – is allocated a hole, and when a resource item is catalogued the relevant holes on the card are notched so it becomes a V-shape rather than a hole. In sorting, a long needle is pushed through the relevant hole in a batch of cards, and the cards with notches drop out. (There are more complex coding systems than the one I have described here. These systems use two or more holes for each item of information, and they permit many more categories of information to be stored in the system.)

A powerful aid to cataloguing is the micro-computer, and there are several data bases available which can be used for cataloguing resources. The data base program allows the user to describe any item in the resource in terms of a set of relevant categories – called 'fields' in the technical jargon. For example, a resource consisting entirely of listening materials might be entered into a data base using the following fields:

- Topic (this might be the name of a unit, or brief title)
- Author (if it comes from a course, for example)
- Course (the name of the course, or if from some other source, this would be left blank)
- Source (this would include the publisher if it is a course, or whatever source the materials came from)
- Type (the person entering data would choose between cassette and tape)
- Channel (choose one or more from spontaneous; authentic; scripted; dialogue; monologue)
- Description (drama; poetry; lecture; ... etc.)
- Activities (listen only; questions; activities)
- Length (long > 8 minutes; medium 4–8 minutes; short < 4 minutes)
- Speed of speech (fast; medium; slow)
- Listening purposes (general information; gist; attitude ... etc.)

(See Appendix C for additional categories.)

Once entered, the data can be used in several ways, and this is the great advantage of a computer data base. Thus, items can be found which fall into one or several categories: so if a user wanted authentic monologues on Topic C with questions, these 'search parameters' could be entered, and the computer would create a separate file containing only items which met these criteria. This information could be read from the screen or printed out. In addition, many data bases will enable the user to carry out various statistical procedures on the data.

The major advantages of computer-based catalogues include the following:

- Any item need only be entered once, yet it can be inserted in several listings from that single entry.

- It is possible to search for items which meet specified criteria.
- It is possible to create lists of items according to relevant categories (for example, all lectures, all items with questions, all items in American English, and so on).
- It is possible to print out these lists on to sheets of paper or on to file cards.

There are two major disadvantages. The first is that in order to get this information from the data base the user has to learn to perform some quite complicated operations. Secondly, only one person can use the computer at any one time; so if there are four or five students seeking information it may take quite a long time for them all to get it. These disadvantages are so serious as to make one doubt the feasibility of using a single micro-computer to catalogue a resource.

However, Michael Carrier of the Davies School in Cambridge (personal communication) has worked out a neat solution to these problems. He uses a micro-computer to record and store the catalogue information on the self-access resource, but the information is printed out on to cards and sheets of paper, which the students use to get the information they require about materials. Thus all the 6–8,000 items in the resource are entered into a data base, and from that source several different catalogues are produced – card catalogues of author and title, and catalogues printed on to sheets of paper and placed in ring binders listing the materials by 'learning purpose'. Carrier, then, exploits the great advantages of the computer but avoids the disadvantages listed above.

6.4 Introduction to the resources

It is very important that learners are given the opportunity, and helped, to learn how to use the self-access resource system. If this is not done successfully, then there will be few users and the number of those may drop off rather drastically. The degree and level of preparation which users need depends on how sophisticated they are in using libraries and similar resources. Most learners, especially adults, will be familiar with libraries, but not all. Anyone considering using resource based learning in the less privileged areas of the world must reckon with the possible unfamiliarity of the learners with library systems. Cousin (1985) warns that an important requirement of successful resource based learning is the sophistication of the learners. 'They must be accustomed to finding their way around a resource, which may require familiarity with the use of a public library, for instance. They must obviously be sufficiently fluent readers to be able to make use of a considerable amount of written instructions and must have the self discipline and habits of study to be able to concentrate on an academic task without outside supervision. It seems unlikely that this is to be achieved without experience of formal education' (para 9).

Even when users of a resource are experienced library users, they still need to be informed about the way that the self-access resource operates. If the self-access mode is used in conjunction with a more traditional class organisation in the institution, then initial induction can be carried out through each class being brought to the resource centre and told about the way it operates. This is unlikely to be sufficient in itself and will need to be supplemented with things like prominently displayed posters giving information about the way the materials are laid out, how to use the listening facilities and so on. It may be advisable to have an area of the resource for notice boards and the display of information. Blake (1982:51) advises that this area should be as professional looking as possible, with posters prepared with a dry print system like Letraset, and instructions typed on a good typewriter and displayed in plastic envelopes to keep them neat and clean.

Where learners are largely independent of class organisation and use only a self-instructional mode, then one must be careful to offer full information on the way the system operates. In the Cambridge Open Access Sound and Video Library users are confronted with a large chart of the layout of the library on the outside door. The potential user's attention is focused on the location of the 'Square One Kit' and on the Catalogue by red dots. The 'Square One Kit' – for first-time users – is located in the foyer to the library and is a folder which contains all the information necessary to use the library efficiently, presented in a self-explanatory form (see figure 27 Harding-Esch 1982:14).

A useful way of assisting users of a self-access centre is to standardise the layout and rubrics used in all in-house materials. In the Audio Centre at the Bell College, Saffron Walden, each cassette has an associated folder which has a work card telling the student what he needs and what he has to do. It may also contain additional materials like worksheet, question sheet, transcript etc. (Brown 1980:21). Preparing learners to use the catalogue can be done through using a quiz which helps them to become familiar with the layout. For example:

You want to listen to this week's news:
- Where will you look?
- What is the colour code?
- What level is it?
- Is there a worksheet for it?
- Where will you look to find out?

Use	Very first contact	To take away	For use in the foyer	For use in the laboratory		To take away if decision to join is made
Elements	Contents description	Leaflet 1	Leaflet 2	Demo cassette 1	Demo cassette + script 2	Feedback sheet
Function	Lead in	General information about library + elements of needs analysis	Specific information on catalogue organisation	Learning how machines operate	Learning how to make use of authentic documents	Feed back to the system

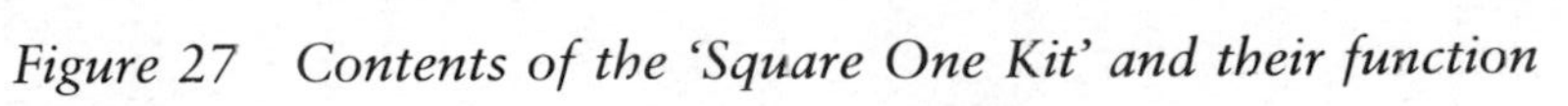

Figure 27 Contents of the 'Square One Kit' and their function

Questions can also be designed to draw learners' attention to specific activities. For example:

You are reading a book called *Running Blind.* You want to listen to it on cassette at the same time. Is this possible? What is the colour code?

Morsman (1980:25)

6.5 The operation of the system

There are several decisions that have to be made about how the system will operate from the user's point of view. We have already supposed that the resource will be self-access, that is, when students can select recorded and printed materials directly from shelves or drawers without necessary help from a teacher or librarian. (This is not, of course, a requirement of self-instruction. For example, the Sound and Video Library at the University of Nancy II is not self-access.) Whatever system is used it is necessary to have some way of keeping track of the material. If a piece of material is not in use, it should be on the shelf or in the drawer indicated by the classification system in the catalogue. If it is in use, there should be some way for the person in charge of the centre and for users to find out who is using it. Big libraries, of course, use a ticket system to keep track of their materials. Such a system is likely to be too complicated for a small resource centre, but there are simpler alternatives. One neat way is to issue each user with three or four cards, or maybe empty cassette boxes, bearing her name and, in the case of the cards, perhaps space to write in a title, date and time. When the user borrows an item she writes the title on her card, having crossed off the titles of previously borrowed items, and writes in the date and time. The card is put in place of the borrowed item. In this way, another user who wants the same item knows that it is being used – rather than misplaced, for example – knows who is using it, and when she began using it.

Another possibility is the 'on the spot copying system'. This has the advantage that a learner does not have to wait for the material she wants, but has the disadvantage that it is only useful for in-house materials on which there are no copyright restrictions. In this system, the user has access to either the catalogue, which must contain fairly complete information, or to master copies of worksheets, and to cassette boxes containing full information. Having selected the printed or audio recorded material she wants to work on, the learner tells the person in charge – a teacher or a technician – who photocopies the sheet, and/or produces a copy of the cassette on a fast copier. The time delay in getting a recording can be reduced, first, by keeping a stock of copies of popular tapes, and secondly by using short cassettes (C15) for the majority of the recordings. An important advantage of this system is that it can easily be extended into home use. Students can have in-house material copied onto their cassettes, and get photocopies of worksheets to use at home.

It goes without saying that whatever system is used, the master copies of tapes, cassettes and worksheets must be kept in a place where there is access only by authorised persons. In this way fresh copies can be made of cassettes and so on that get lost or damaged.

Finally the self-access system should be simple to use for both learners and tutors. Both will want to get information about the materials, and in addition, tutors may need to use it to enter new materials. If this is a complicated or lengthy process, new materials may not be entered up very quickly, or may get into the resource without getting catalogued at all, and so get lost. Secondly, sometimes several people want to use the catalogue at the same time. If there is only one micro-computer, and a long queue of people waiting to use it, they might not appreciate its qualities and wish for a return to the old fashioned card index system which can be used by a number of people simultaneously. One way of ensuring that the system is easy to use is to have a single member of staff who can take special responsibility for developing it and encouraging others to develop it; and for organising and indexing it. It is clear that this is not a job which can be done in addition to a full teaching load, and that such a person needs time off from teaching to do the job.

6.6 Evaluation

The success of a self-access resource centre will depend largely on how well it meets the needs of the users, how 'user friendly' it is, whether there are the appropriate materials in sufficient quantities and so on. The people who know whether there is enough information, whether they are able to find the materials they are looking for, and generally whether the place is operating smoothly, are the users. It makes sense then, to try to tap this information. Just chatting to users about the system will certainly give you some impressions, but these need to be recorded to be useful at a time when the staff have the leisure to make changes. However, the users who make comments about the system may not be typical, and so collecting written feedback from all the users is worth the effort. Blake (1982:51) suggests that the students' cards left in place of a cassette or book borrowed from the shelves can double as a feedback device. These cards could have questions typed on them assessing the usefulness of the piece of material borrowed, and more general questions about its accessibility and so on. Such written information is useful in deciding on whether the system is operating efficiently; and it provides the basis for statistics on users and so on. These may be useful when you are trying to persuade your institution to give you more money to expand the facility.

6.7 Conclusion

Although self-access resources are not essential to self-instruction, this is a convenient and flexible way of organising the learning resources, and it makes it easier to deal with learners who have diverse requirements. Establishing a basic self-access resource centre could be done adequately for the same cost as establishing a 20-place language laboratory. Indeed a number of the existing centres came about in this way, the staff deciding not to replace a language laboratory, but to use the money for a more flexible arrangement. Like much concerned with self-instruction, the use of a self-access resource requires that the learners have adequate preparation. The question of preparation for self-instruction generally is the topic of the next chapter.

7 Preparing for self-instruction

Both learners and teachers may need preparation to undertake self-instruction and this chapter discusses the possible types of preparation and suggests some techniques which can be used to provide it.

7.1 Types of preparation

Both Holec and Riley of CRAPEL distinguish between *psychological* preparation and *practical* or *methodological* preparation. Holec (1980:27) writes of psychological preparation as a gradual 'deconditioning process' through which the learner can free himself from many kinds of assumptions and prejudices about learning languages: for example, that there is one ideal method and that teachers possess it; that the learner's knowledge of the mother tongue is of no use to him for learning a foreign language; that his knowledge of, and experience of learning other subjects is not useful in language learning; that he is not capable of making any valid assessment of his performance, and so on. Psychological preparation, then, can be seen as a process of developing self-confidence among learners in their ability to work independently of the teacher, and of developing a different attitude towards language learning – essentially that of self-direction.

Psychological preparation is concerned first with persuading learners to try self-instruction, secondly with facilitating a change of attitude about language learning away from false assumptions and prejudices, and thirdly with helping learners to build their self-confidence in their ability to work independently of the teacher.

The same three components of psychological preparation may be useful for teachers too, especially in situations where a self-instructional mode has been adopted without the full agreement of all the teachers in an institution, or where teachers are newly recruited to institutions using a self-instructional mode. So some teachers may need to be persuaded that self-instruction is a viable mode. Secondly, some may need to be weaned away from the same kinds of false assumptions and prejudices which beset many learners. And thirdly they may also need to build their confidence that learners are capable of undertaking a great deal of responsibility for their own learning, and they may need to build up their self-confidence in being able to adopt the new roles necessary in a self-instructional learning mode.

The best way to achieve these objectives for both learners and teachers is through successful practice. Thus the best way to convince someone that self-instruction is worth a try is to give them a successful experience of it, and the best way to build a learner's self-confidence in his ability to work independently of the teacher is likewise to give him successful experience of so working. Similarly, the best way to free people from false assumptions and prejudices about language learning is to demonstrate their falsity. Consequently, psychological preparation and methodological preparation should ideally go on simultaneously. However, there are circumstances where this is not possible – where for instance the learners are so sceptical about self-instruction or so reluctant to try it that this would affect the results of a trial experience.

For Riley (1980) 'methodological preparation is to psychological preparation what showing is to telling', and he adds that people who are not particuarly impressed by the kind of abstract arguments that may be used as part of psychological preparation may nevertheless see the practical value of particular activities. Methodological preparation for the learner is the process of acquiring the abilities and techniques he needs to undertake self-instruction. It is a matter first of becoming aware of learning processes and techniques which learners operate implicitly, and then combining this knowledge with certain skills more usually expected in teachers than in learners.

For the teacher, methodological preparation involves recognising the necessary changes of role of teachers working in a self-instructional mode, and learning the new skills such role changes demand.

7.2 Preparing teachers

A self-instructional learning mode does not require fewer teachers, nor does it result in teachers having less work, though it may mean that the teachers' roles and relationships change. This is not surprising when one considers what is demanded from the teacher working in this mode. Tough (1979:181) lists the salient characteristics of the ideal 'helper' – based on research done in the late 1960s. ('Helper' is a term sometimes used in preference to teacher – to emphasise the *helping* role.)

The ideal helper is warm and loving. He accepts and cares about the learner and about his problems, and takes them seriously. He is willing to spend time helping. He is approving, supportive, encouraging and friendly; and he regards the learner as an equal. As a result of these characteristics, the learner feels free to approach him and can talk freely and easily with him in a warm and relaxed atmosphere.

A second group of characteristics concerns the helper's perception of the learner's capacity to plan and undertake his own learning. The ideal helper has confidence in the learner's ability to make appropriate plans and arrangements for his learning. He has a high regard for the learner's skill in planning his own work, and does not want to take away from him control of the decision making. As a result of this perception, the helper views his interaction with the learner as a dialogue; his help will be tailored to the needs, goals and requests of the learner, and the helper listens, understands, accepts and responds as well as helps. This is in contrast to those helpers who want to control, command, manipulate, persuade, influence and change the learner. Such a helper views the learner as an object, and expects to do something *to* that object. This is reminiscent of the research cited in Chapter 2 from Bockman and Bockman (1972) which suggested that learners are liable to fulfil the prophecies made of their ability to undertake responsibility for their own learning.

Tough's list of the personal qualities and attitudes of the ideal helper must be extended in terms of professional knowledge and skills required of a helper of language learners. The following list is adapted from Carver (1982a:33) and McCafferty (ND:22). The ideal helper requires knowledge and skills in:

- *the learners' mother tongues* in order to be able to communicate with the learners without difficulty and with a minimum risk of misunderstandings;
- *the target language* in order to help the learner with all or most of the items below;
- *needs analysis*, to help the learner to identify and describe his needs in language learning;
- *setting objectives* in order to help the learner to break down these needs into achievable objectives;
- *linguistic analysis* in order to identify for the learner (and later to help the learner identify for himself) the key learning points in authentic texts in subject areas relevant to learners with specific language requirements;
- *materials* in order to help the learner to find appropriate materials from the resources in the institution, but this would also include knowledge of published materials in order to help build up the resource;
- *materials preparation* in order to prepare appropriate materials from authentic texts, and in order to adapt published and in-house materials for self-instruction;
- *assessment procedures* in order to help learners to assess their proficiency and to develop self-assessment techniques;

- *learning strategies* in order to advise learners about the best ways for them to go about their learning, and in order to be able to recommend alternatives to learners who are not succeeding;
- *management and administration* in order to maintain lists of native speakers of the target language(s), find other learners of the target language(s) and arrange meetings among learners, arrange learning exchanges, monitor learners and keep records of them;
- *librarianship* in order to establish, maintain and run the self-access resources centre; this may include skills in cataloguing (perhaps using a micro-computer), devising and operating ways of keeping track of resources and being responsible for ordering new materials.

It would be very optimistic to expect to find an individual who possessed all of these qualities and skills; nevertheless all are desirable among the staff of an institution offering supported self-instructional learning. A programme of preparation for tutors should be concerned first to identify people with various of these skills and qualities, and secondly with helping tutors to acquire as many of them as is feasible.

7.2.1 Psychological and methodological preparation of teachers

Teachers, like learners, may need both psychological and methodological preparation. Those who are new to self-instruction, those who lack confidence in themselves to help learners in this mode, and those who are doubtful or sceptical about self-instruction may benefit from a programme of workshops, enabling them to consider and reflect on this instructional mode, and the arguments and evidence in support of it. The major objectives of such preparation would include giving participants an opportunity to discover the full breadth of possible meanings of the concept of self-instruction; to reflect on their own attitudes to this instructional mode; and to consider the necessary changes of role and task required of the teacher who is helping learners working in a self-instructional mode. Suggestions for workshops which meet these objectives are given in Appendix B. Suitable *methodological* preparation is mainly a matter of learning about the methodological preparation required by the learners in order that teachers can help to prepare groups of learners. Teachers can then apply the teaching skills they already possess to the new content. Appendix C(I) offers suggestions about the methodological preparation of learners.

It is likely that, in spite of preparatory workshops, some teachers will remain unconvinced and feel unhappy in working in this way. It goes without saying that it would be wrong to force change upon them, as it would be wrong to force learners into self-instruction. There is unlikely to be any shortage of need for conventional class teachers, even where self-instruction has an important role.

7.3 Preparing adult learners

An important factor that we have to take into account in our discussion of preparation for self-instruction is the amount of time available for it. Children, and some groups of adults, are engaged in a language learning programme which may last for a number of years, and so their preparation can be both more extensive and less intense than those learners who have only a short period available for language learning. Consequently we will make the distinction between those learners who have time only for the *minimum* necessary preparation and those who have time for *extended preparation*. Preparing learners for self-instruction always takes time, often from a tight learning schedule. Obviously we must limit the training to fit the time available, and to suit the requirements of groups and individuals. However, it is important to remember that for learners beyond the beginning stage at least, these activities can constitute valuable authentic practice in using the target language to communicate, and they can be presented partly as activities to practise communication. They are particularly valuable in that the content is highly meaningful to the learners.

7.3.1 Techniques for psychological preparation

There are several activities that can be used for giving psychological preparation, and a number of examples are given in Appendix C(I). They have two main objectives: to help learners to come to terms with their feelings about self-instruction – their anxieties and their aspirations for it; and to demonstrate the feasibility of self-instruction as a learning mode by getting the participants to undertake a small learning project through self-instruction. The amount of psychological preparation required will vary from group to group depending on their readiness to undertake this learning mode. With learners who have time only for minimal preparation, it may be necessary to curtail this to a short talk, and depend on the demonstration through methodological preparation to convince those that are sceptical. For learners who are engaged in an extensive learning programme on the other hand, it is desirable to spread this preparation out over a period, mixed with methodological preparation.

All language learners need to feel that their learning is purposeful to be successful. Purposefulness is, at least in part, dependent on the structuring of the learning – the identification of relevant objectives, their assembly into a realistic learning programme, the encouragement of the learner to meet the deadlines in the programme, and the provision of some means to inform the learner whether he is achieving his objectives. This structuring is conventionally external to the learners, and the factor which represents the greatest difference between a self-instructional mode of learning and a more teacher-centred mode is the degree to which the language learning work is subject to external structuring. Knowles (1975:37) warns that many learners 'enter into a new learning situation feeling a deep need for the security of a clear structural plan – an outline, course syllabus, time schedule and the like.' In addition they want to feel that their teachers know what they are doing and are in charge of the learning situation. This is clearly a significant matter which must be taken account of in any programme of psychological preparation.

The solution which Knowles adopts is to emphasise that the self-instructional work will be within a structure, but one of a different kind from those which the learners have been used to. This new kind he describes as a *process structure*, that is, a structure deriving from the way of learning rather than the content. In a self-instructional mode the content will vary according to the individual's needs and interests, but the process by which the content is acquired is structured in terms of devices such as needs analysis techniques, self-assessment techniques, and most important of all, the learner contract. Knowles assures the learners that he is in charge of the process in the initial stages, and that he will make decisions about the procedures when the learners are not in a position to make decisions for themselves. And he assures the learners that he knows what he is doing.

7.3.2 Methodological preparation

We said above that methodological preparation was a matter of the learner first becoming consciously aware of learning processes and techniques which he operates implicitly, and then combining this knowledge with certain skills more usually expected in teachers than learners. A useful framework for this is the model proposed by Nisbet and Shucksmith (1984:8) which distinguishes the following three levels:

- *Approach to learning*, which is concerned with the 'intelligent regulation of learning';
- *Learning plans*, which are concerned with 'superordinate skills, generalised procedures or sequences of activities with a conscious purpose';
- *Learning skills*, which are skills specific to subjects.

If we insert into this framework the knowledge and techniques needed by an autonomous self-instructing learner, the following hierarchical model results, with a set of actual 'learning to learn' objectives ordered from the more general to the more specific, which can be used as the basis of a programme of methodological preparation (see figure 28).

The skills and abilities under set 1, *Approach to learning*, are concerned with general education and learning rather than specifically with language learning. The objectives deriving from these are likely to arise through general education rather than through a programme of preparation, though preparation may be useful in fine tuning some of them. Thus, for example, objective 1.3, 'The ability to translate learning needs into learning objectives', can be improved through training. Set 2, *Learning plans*, are directly related to language learning, but are at a higher level of generality than specific learning techniques. Here then, we are concerned with procedures generally useful in self-instructional language learning, being involved with such matters as the completion of a language contract, the use of a self-access resource and the ability to undertake self-assessment. These are matters which are amenable to preparation and which would constitute part of any thorough programme of preparation. Finally, set 3, *Learning skills*, is concerned with actual learning techniques which must be learned by those entering into a self-instructional learning mode.

The immediate use we can make of this table is to provide a principled basis for distinguishing between *minimum* necessary preparation and *extended* preparation. Those learners who have time only for minimum preparation will concentrate on set 3, *Learning skills*, whereas other learners with more time available can be given preparation in set 2, *Learning plans*. The general education offered to school learners and maybe some adult learners would hopefully aim to develop the abilities in set 1 also.

To an extent, learner preparation is concerned with helping all learners to develop those attitudes and skills that we suppose good learners bring to language learning. In Chapter 2 we cited Stern's view of the basic strategies likely to be adopted by good learners. These were:

- *An active planning strategy* concerned with matters like the selection of goals and the identification of stages of learning.
- *An academic (explicit) learning strategy* involving matters directly involved with language learning; that is, analysis, practice, memorisation and monitoring.
- *A social learning strategy* concerned with the learner's attempts to find opportunities for authentic language practice.
- *An effective strategy* concerned with the emotional and motivational problems of language learning.

	Examples of actual learning to learn objectives
1 *Approach to learning* – Intelligent regulation of learning, self-monitoring, selection of strategies, insight through reflection	1.1 The ability to decide what knowledge and skills to learn 1.2 The ability to diagnose learning needs realistically 1.3 The ability to translate learning needs into learning objectives 1.4 The ability to identify resources – both human and material 1.5 The ability to allocate and organise time for learning
2 *Learning plans* – Superordinate skills, generalised procedures or sequences of activities with a conscious purpose	2.1 The ability to apply other skills and knowledge to the completion of learning contracts, etc. 2.2 The ability to determine task objectives (e.g. what to use a particular reading/listening passage for) 2.3 The ability to undertake self-assessment 2.4 The ability to use course materials to help maintain language learning objectives 2.5 The ability to use reference materials (dictionaries, grammar books etc.) to help attain language learning objectives 2.6 The ability to use self-access learning systems (e.g. learning resources, libraries, etc.) 2.7 The ability to work co-operatively with others to achieve learning objectives 2.8 The ability to use human resources to help attain language learning objectives etc.
3 *Learning skills* – Skills specific to particular aspects of language learning, e.g. reading for information, oral communication for transactional purposes, etc.	3.1 Selecting learning techniques 3.2 Devising exercises 3.3 Doing exercises 3.4 Monitoring performance – written and spoken 3.5 Applying criteria of assessment 3.6 Administering self-tests etc.

Figure 28 Methodological preparation

Wesche (1979:426) observed and interviewed good learners. She reports that her research results

> suggest that most successful learners, while differing in their particular learning techniques and L2 practice activities, are those who use their exposure time in the L2 actively, and who seek to extend this out of the classroom; who actively rehearse new material; who exploit its rich associational possibilities both through conscious association-making and meaningful practice in the L2; and who seek knowledge about the target language. They are characterised by a high level of personal initiative and sustained effort in the language learning process, which appears to be related to a long term commitment to mastery of the L2.

Certain of these strategies can be taught directly, and it may be that some of the attitudes can be developed through helping learners to a greater awareness of language in general, and of the processes of communication in language. Two recent movements in language teaching are attempting to give learners greater preparation for language learning. A recent development of modern language teaching in Britain (at least) is language awareness training, one facet of which is to heighten the learner's awareness about the nature of language, and about the nature of communication and of the nature of language learning. The intended outcomes of these programmes include knowledge of a metalanguage; a realisation that there is much in common between the mother tongue and the foreign language; and a greater understanding and consciousness on the part of the learner of his own learning processes.

The second movement advocates a programme of 'learner training' for all language learners. Proponents argue that at least one difference between good language learners and the rest is that good learners have developed effective learning strategies. It may be the case, the argument goes on, that if we were to train all learners in a selection of the strategies used by good learners, then they would improve the efficiency of their learning.

Rubin (1981) and Cohen and Aphek (1981) investigated the strategies learners use in their learning and offer valuable lists – from which it would be possible to construct programmes of learner training.

Successful speakers are willing to talk and to make errors in the foreign language. They make decisions about when they want to be corrected, and about what use they make of the corrections. They paraphrase what native speakers say. They check that their listeners are following what they are saying by using techniques such as asking the listener for a word – which the listener could only supply if he was following the discourse (Cohen). Rubin suggests that good learners create opportunities for practising the language by, for example, initiating conversations with target language speakers, including fellow students and the teacher. They consciously use communication strategies while speaking. Thus they get their message across by using circumlocution and paraphrase. They use synonyms of particular words, cognates (whether they are right or wrong), gestures, and they may even spell out or write a word to make the meaning clear. Similarly they use strategies to maintain the conversation. So they use 'formulaic' utterances (that is, phrases or sentences such as greetings and apologies which are memorised as wholes); they direct the conversation to areas in which they have greater knowledge of appropriate language.

Successful listeners make use of all available information to interpret the input. Thus they use their knowledge of the given topic and other knowledge of the world they have available. They use cues from prior utterances within the discourse, cues from word stress and their knowledge of the speaker, the tone of voice, and the speaker's body language. They create interactions and so maximise their opportunity to listen to the target language, and they take an active part by asking for clarifications of meaning, meanings of words and so on. They check their own understanding by summarising the content of the exchange (Cohen).

Techniques used to memorise vocabulary by successful learners include the following (Cohen and Aphek 1981):

- associating the structure of part or all of a word with a known word in the target language (for example, Hebrew *lifney* 'before' to *lifamin* 'sometimes', *seder* 'order' to *leseder* 'to order')
- associating the sound of a new word with the sound of a word in the mother tongue, or the target language or some other language (for example *benatayim* 'meanwhile' associated with *ben* to *beyn* 'between' and *tayim* to 'time')
- meaning of part or all of a word
- mental image of a word
- situation in which the word occurred
- physical sensation associated with the word
- visualising the word
- grouping words according to the similarity of endings

Good learners develop techniques for clarifying meaning and understanding (Rubin 1981). Thus they are active in making use of the teacher or other informant to clarify their understanding. They ask for examples of how to use particular words or expressions, for translations into the mother tongue, for repetitions, for the meaning of the item, for the difference in meaning between two items, for a paraphrase, and ask about the application of known rules to the item. Such learners will also repeat the word, and/or put it into a sentence to confirm understanding; or repeat part of the word or phrase, and ask for the remainder.

They use various guessing strategies to get to meaning. They use clues such as the other items in the sentence; the syntactic structure; the context and topic of discourse; any visual clues. Successful learners use various deductive reasoning techniques to develop their understanding of the structure of the target language. Thus they compare the target language with their mother tongue or another known language to identify regular similarities and differences, and they infer grammatical rules by analogy.

Good learners develop successful techniques for practice and memorisation. They practise with new sounds both in isolation and in context, they pronounce out loud and may use a mirror for practice. They practise intonation contours by using such techniques as chaining – progressively lengthening a sentence, as in the following example:

– a *type*writer
– a nice *type*writer
– a very nice *type*writer
– a very nice black *type*writer

They talk to anyone available in the new language, and if no one is available they talk to themselves, consciously applying grammatical rules and making use of new words.

Good learners actively monitor their own and other people's performance. Thus, they correct errors in pronunciation, spelling, grammar and style. They observe and analyse the language use of others to see how the message was interpreted by the addressee. They also note the source of their own errors – interference from the mother tongue, or from another second language.

Successful learners use the following reading strategies:

– They choose a reading approach appropriate to the given text and their purpose in reading it.
– They summarise as they go along.
– They read for general meaning rather than for literal meaning.
– They adopt 'fuzzy processing' in that they tolerate vague meaning until they can clarify the meaning. They use dictionaries sparingly.
– They use syntactic processing as a last resort.

Successful learners use the following writing strategies:

– They adopt a cyclical process of planning, writing and reviewing.
– They read over what they have just written before proceeding to the next paragraph or other section.

– They write for meaning first.
– They are prepared to produce multiple drafts of their written material.

7.4 Preparing school learners

Self-instruction could be promoted in schools by introducing specific innovations into the language programme and into the activities in the classroom. However, such an approach would risk rejection by many teachers since, quite naturally, their primary objective is working through the syllabus and preparing their pupils for the examinations. Consequently, the approach recommended here is to use the tasks and activities normally undertaken by pupils and teachers in the classroom, and to promote self-instruction and autonomy through them.

Such well-known activities as group and pair work, and the use of project work with its consequent focusing on interesting and meaningful (even maybe useful) content are all useful in giving the learner the opportunity to take greater responsibility for his own learning. In addition there are several techniques, activities and procedures which can be adopted into the classroom without a lot of disruption and which will greatly enhance this preparation towards autonomy. These and several other techniques are discussed in detail in Carver and Dickinson (1982).

School learners can be encouraged to monitor their own learning. This may be as simple as keeping a check-list of items covered, or it may, with older and more sophisticated learners, involve keeping a learning diary which could include a check-list, a self-rating on how well the items were learned and, perhaps, a record of areas of difficulty and what was done about them. Learners can be encouraged to take every opportunity to correct their own work as an introduction to self-assessment; and they can be given training in designing, and opportunities to design their own learning materials, as an introduction to working on authentic materials. (See Appendix D(I).)

Taking the pupils into your confidence by sharing with them the kind of information about objectives and activities available to the teacher, but not usually to the pupils, helps them to begin the process of planning their own learning. Thus the teacher might explain briefly at the beginning of each unit what he has planned to do, and why he has chosen to do those activities. A further step would be to invite pupils to make suggestions about things they would like to do. The teacher might state the objectives in terms of targets for the pupils' learning over the next period of time. For example, the teacher might say:

'By the end of this unit you should be able to refuse an invitation by saying

– Thank you very much
– I'd love to
– That's very kind of you

} but ....'

The teacher can begin preparation of pupils making their own contracts by indicating minimum objectives to be achieved in the ordinary classroom lessons (such things as 'Score at least seven out of ten; read at least three books by the end of the term; learn the dialogue by heart') so that even weak learners have a sense of achievement. At the same time, further objectives can be indicated (for example, 'Go on to answer level II questions; read another three books, or read three by the middle of the term', and so on). The next stage is to encourage learners to draw up their own objectives, perhaps by contracting with the teacher to do such and such by a particular time.

Trouble shooting is another activity which involves confidences; but this time it is the pupils who take the teacher into their confidence. In trouble shooting sessions the teacher tries to get the learners to become aware of their learning problems by getting them to talk about them.

There is no doubt but that some of these activities are time consuming, for example the process of sharing objectives with the learners, or explaining what the objectives are, and perhaps encouraging the learners to contribute their own objectives, takes up valuable time. However, such activities are likely to have a very positive influence by improving motivation, and so improving efficiency of learning.

7.5 Conclusion

We have been concerned in this chapter with examining the preparation which is needed by both learners and teachers who are new to self-instruction. In both cases, psychological and methodological preparation are needed. Psychological preparation on the teacher's part is largely concerned with adapting to the change of role necessary in self-instruction.

For learners it was suggested that besides the preparation necessary simply to use the materials and resources available, learners might benefit from a programme of learner training which would introduce them to the learning strategies used by good learners.

A very important aspect of preparation is that required for self-assessment. This topic is touched upon in the present chapter, but dealt with in detail in the following one.

8 Self-assessment

The very idea of self-assessment is a contradiction in terms. How can an individual learner be expected to take an objective view of his or her own attainment without succumbing to the temptation to cheat? The whole idea is ridiculous!

Participant in a seminar

In one sense the speaker quoted above is right, or at least many language teachers would strongly agree with him. When assessment is used for certification, self-assessment does not seem to have a part to play. When an institution such as an examinations body – the Cambridge Examinations Board, or the Royal Society of Arts for example, or a University or a College – certify that a person has a particular level of proficiency in a language, then it is clear that the tests or examinations leading to certification should be designed, conducted and evaluated by appropriately qualified people who can be completely objective about the test and the results.

In another sense the speaker quoted above is less clearly right. Many language learners – and one suspects, most successful language learners – regularly engage in self-assessment as part of their learning. They do exercises, and check, by whatever means available, whether their responses are correct or not. They write passages in the foreign language and monitor the correctness and appropriateness of the language used. They construct simple tests of vocabulary. They assess their understanding of reading passages. They check other people's comprehension of their spoken language, and adjust it when necessary. These are all examples of self-assessment in one sense of the term. The differences between this and earlier senses lie in such things as:

- Formality. These examples of self-assessment are all very informal.
- The use to which the assessment is put. Formal assessment is usually used for certification, while self-assessment is usually used by the learner to get information about her learning.
- Who requires the information. This is perhaps where the most significant difference lies. A learner may have a pretty good idea of her own level of communicative ability; demonstrating a representative sample of it in a relatively short time to someone else requires a sophisticated test.

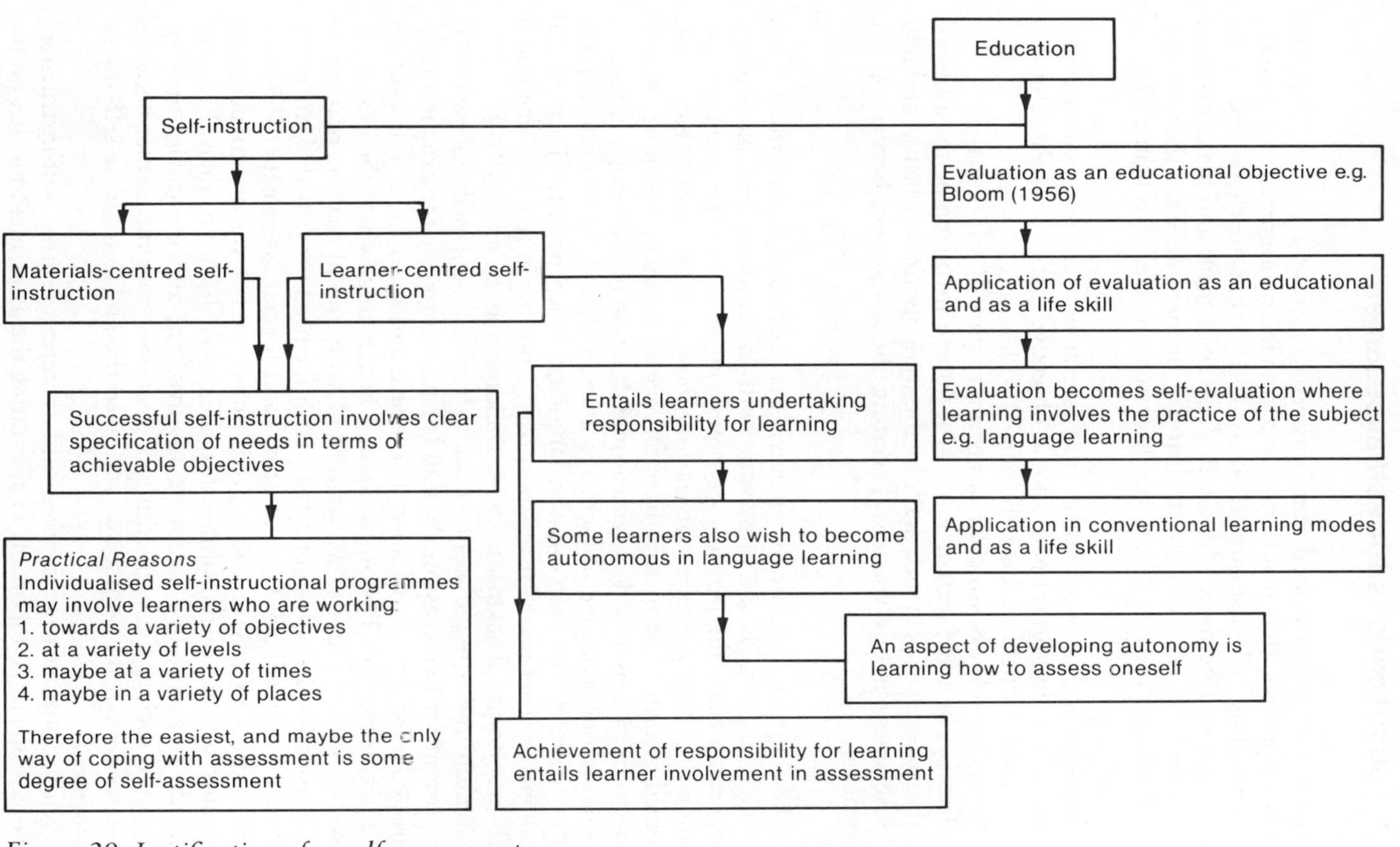

Figure 29 Justifications for self-assessment

8.1 Justifications for self-assessment

Even if it is demonstrated that learners *can* make acceptably accurate self-assessments, that would not be a convincing argument for actually implementing self-assessment. It is likely that teachers and other specialists will be more reliable in their assessment and make accurate assessments more often than the learners themselves. Why, then, recommend self-assessment? There are three reasons (see also figure 29):

- The first and most general is that assessment leading towards evaluation is an important educational objective in its own right, and that training learners in this is beneficial to learning.
- Secondly, self-assessment is a necessary part of self-direction.
- Thirdly, in a self-instructional programme involving many students, the assessment demands made by the students are very heavy, and self-assessment is one way of alleviating the assessment burden on the teacher.

The ability to evaluate the effectiveness of one's own performance in a foreign language is an important skill in learning, and particularly important when the learning becomes autonomous. The point of education as partly a process of learning how to learn is one that I have argued elsewhere with specific reference to language learning. A language course can only deal with a small fraction of the foreign language; therefore one objective of language courses should be to teach learners how to carry on learning the language independently. Part of the training learners need for this purpose is training in self-assessment and self-monitoring (Dickinson 1974, Dickinson and Carver 1980).

Within the specific context of self-instruction, self-assessment is important for two reasons. Within learner-centred self-instruction (self-directed learning – see Chapter 1 section 2 and figure 29) self-assessment is a necessary part. Decisions about whether to go on to the next item, exercise or unit, decisions concerned with the allocation of time to various skills, decisions concerned with the need for remedial work, are all based on feedback from informal and formal assessment. These are key matters in any learning programme, and if we are to persuade learners to take responsibility for their own learning, then this must include responsibility for being involved in, and eventually making, decisions such as these. In addition, of course, once the learner becomes independent of the course she will need the ability to make self-assessments.

Within both learner-centred and materials-centred self-instruction, self-assessment is important in alleviating the assessment burden on the teacher. Individualised self-instructional programmes may involve many learners who are working towards a variety of language learning objectives at a variety of levels. These factors in themselves are likely to generate a heavy burden of assessment. In addition, the learners may be working at varying, and maybe, unpredictable times, and the learners may not be available for testing at times convenient to the tutor. Self-assessment used for appropriate testing purposes – to provide feedback information, diagnostic testing, and maybe placement testing – can release the tutor for tasks such as counselling, and for assessment tasks that cannot easily be conducted by the learner herself.

8.2 The range of self-assessment

The concept of self-assessment has many facets: assessment is used for many purposes; different age groups have different abilities in self-assessing, and there can be many different degrees of involvement of 'the self' in self-assessment; and so it is important to analyse the concept thoroughly. I shall give examples of self-assessment used in different ways and for different purposes, and then discuss the examples. The examples and the discussion follow the framework presented in figure 30. This sets out to show at a glance what self-assessment includes, and the limits and possibilities in self-assessment.

8.2.1 Learner choice in summative assessment

Some learners are given no choice whatever with regard to assessment (as indeed, some learners are offered no opportunities to take responsibility for their learning). Sometimes this can lead to unhappy consequences.

Example 1 Mustaq Ahmed

> Mustaq Ahmed is one of several students sponsored by his government first to improve his English, and then to train as an English language teacher. Though he has worked very hard, his English is still weak at the end of the first term. The tutor tells the class that the Ministry of Education in the students' country has decided that all the students will take the English as a Second Language Test of the English North West Regional Examinations Board. The oral part of the test, Mustaq Ahmed is told, will take place at the end of the following term. All students are automatically registered for the test; there is no question of choice. Mustaq Ahmed is very anxious; he knows his English is

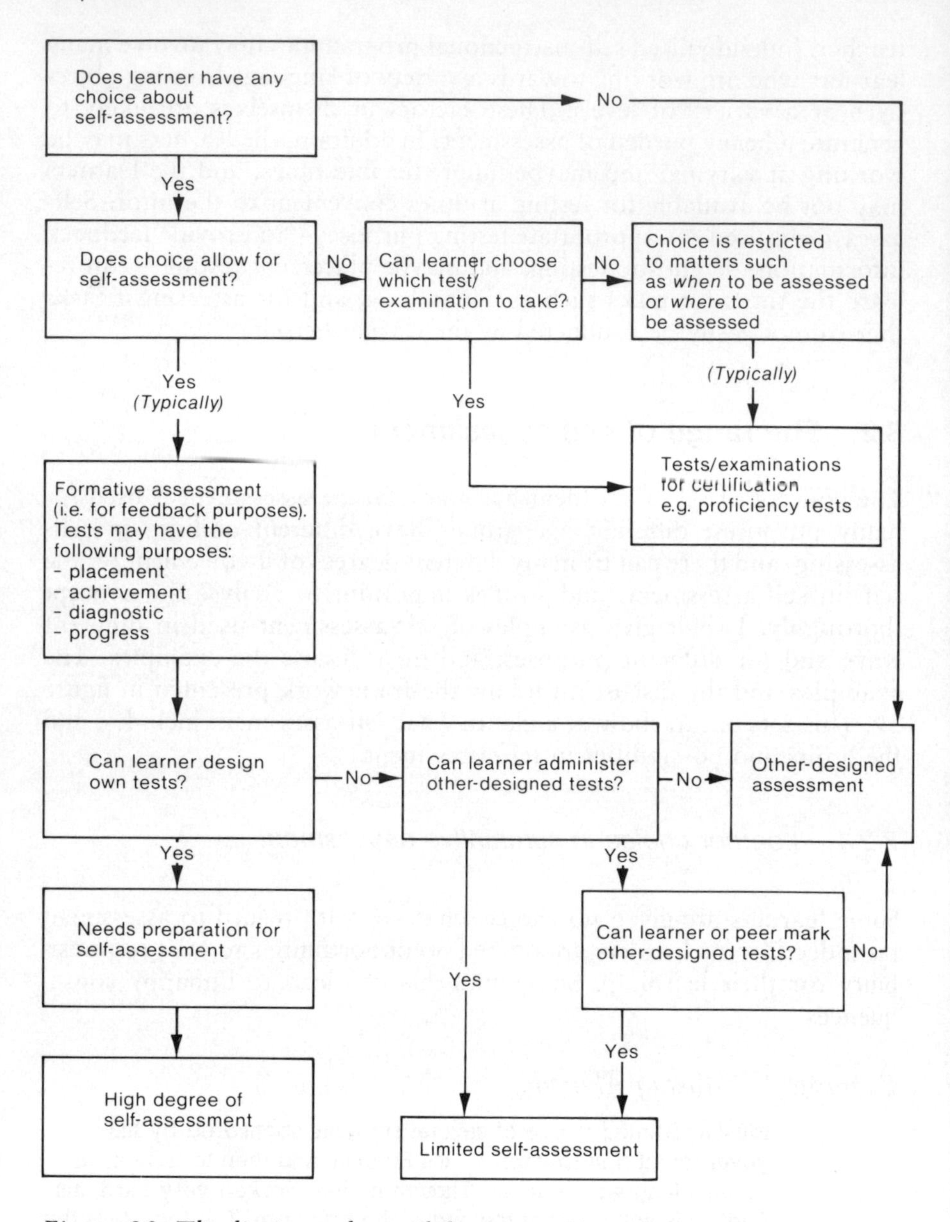

Figure 30 The limits and possibilities in self-assessment

weak, particularly his oral skills, and he fears that he will fail. He does!

Although in the past teachers have tended to discount the contributions learners could make in judging matters like their readiness for a test or examination, this view is now changing, and learners are being drawn into the decision making. By being given some responsibility for these matters, learners are assisted in developing towards autonomy.

Example 2 Marie Lamour

Marie Lamour has come to Britain for a year to improve her English. She enrols for an English course at an adult college and in the second month of the course she learns that it is possible to take the Cambridge First Certificate Examination in English in December. She asks her teacher about it and the teacher confirms that the test is held in December, but she is doubtful about Marie's chances of passing. Marie, however, insists that she wishes to take the exam, and the teacher agrees to register her for it. In the remaining time before the exam Marie works very hard, and when the results come she discovers that she has passed, but only just.

Choosing whether or when to take an examination is the realistic limit of learner choice so far as summative assessment is concerned. This is particularly true where 'certification' is awarded on the basis of the examination, for example the Cambridge Certificate, the General Certificate of Education or the MLA test. However, where the purpose of the test is to provide information about the effectiveness of the learning to the learner (and to others) then self-assessment is a realistic possibility.

8.2.2 Self-assessment for formative assessment purposes

Let us now consider what these possibilities are. The two main ones, shown on figure 30, are that the learner designs her own tests, or that she administers to herself tests that have been designed by others. Following from these there are a number of subsidiary possibilities. Thus, there is the issue of what purpose the tests have – placement, achievement, diagnostic or progress; and there is the question of who marks the tests – the person who has been tested or someone else.

Where tests designed for assessing proficiency are used as a learner/teacher feedback device, as part of the preparation for a public examination for certification, then there is considerable scope for self-assessment. It is relatively common for learners to self-administer tests designed by others, and it is also possible for learners to design their own tests for some skill/ability areas. Learners who self-administer tests designed by others often use past examination papers of the relevant public examination, or published books of tests which claim to be relevant to the examination.

Example 3 Simone Renan (I)

Simone Renan is studying English in Britain and she intends taking the Cambridge Certificate examination in the summer. In addition to the work given to her by the college, she has undertaken a number of self-assessment activities. She has bought a book of tests which claim to be appropriate for the Cambridge Certificate. She does one or two of these per week and checks her responses against the answers in the book. When she is not sure about an answer she asks her teacher at the college to check it. Simone keeps a record of her percentage score, and thinks that over the two months or so she has been doing this that she is getting better.

Such published tests are often weak on 'productive skills' such as continuous writing, since it is difficult to give answers for these. There are possibilities in self-designed tests.

Example 4 Simone Renan (II)

Simone is also a member of a self-help group formed of herself and three or four other students from her class in college. They all regularly write compositions in English, and the group comments on them. Simone has just written her latest composition. After quite a lot of thought and heart searching she has given herself a grade based on criteria which the teacher at the college has supplied (see Appendix D(I)). She will now give photocopies of her composition to other members of the group who will read it and grade it according to the same criteria that Simone herself has used. The group will then discuss her work, each person (including Simone) justifying the grade, and each making at least one suggestion of how the composition might be improved. Simone finds this a very valuable activity; it improves both her writing, and her spoken English skills, and it makes very clear to her the kind of criteria that will be used to grade the examination. Simone's class teacher is very impressed by the activities of the self-help group, and she has resolved to encourage the formation of other self-help groups with her class next year. She is also considering adopting this peer assessment system for at least part of the internal continuous assessment in the course.

Learners need adequate preparation if they are to use this scheme successfully. They need to be convinced of its usefulness, and they may need to learn about criteria and how to use them. One preparation technique is to supply small groups of learners with composition plans, rough drafts and finished drafts that have been previously produced, and give them exercises in applying the criteria to these. Although this preparation will take time from a possibly tight schedule, the students will learn a lot about writing compositions from this activity. Moreover, the discussions, if they can be conducted in the target language, will give excellent, meaningful practice in oral communication.

Assessment used for *placement testing* has elements of certification about it (in reports and references for example: 'John Smith was in the top form throughout his school life'), but also has elements of learner feedback, and on this account a self-assessment mode may be acceptable in some instructional situations.

Example 5 Francis Capaldi

> Francis Capaldi is quite familiar with self-assessment. He had been in Sweden for a year or two before he decided to take classes in Swedish. When he went to the training school, he was given a Self-Assessment Proficiency Inventory which he was asked to fill in. This asked him to make an assessment of his level of competence in Swedish in the various 'skill' areas, and on the basis of this he was placed in a class at a particular level. This was a provisional arrangement, but in his case the self-assessment he had made fitted with the teacher's estimate and so he stayed in that class. A number of his class mates changed classes, some to a lower class, some to a higher.

In the example above the learner is using a test designed by someone else, and he is simply administering it himself. This form of test is not 'marked' since the method of completing it is for the learner to decide where on a scale he would place his level of competence. (See examples from Oskarsson in Appendix D(I), and in Oskarsson 1978.) This kind of test is often referred to as a self-rating questionnaire, and the best known work in these is that of Matts Oskarsson and of Tibor von Elek, both of the Language Teaching Research Centre, University of Gothenburg, Sweden; and that coming from work into Graded Objectives carried out in Britain, particularly the work in Lothian Region* in Scotland done by John Clark and his associates. These are all described and illustrated in Appendix D(I).

* Lothian is a region in the south-east of Scotland, which includes the city of Edinburgh.

Achievement tests are tests which measure a learner's achievement level in terms of a particular course – or module of a course – that the learner has been following. Their main purpose is to give feedback information – and of course the results may be used for placing the individual in an appropriate group. Consequently these tests are also amenable to a self-assessment mode.

Example 6 James Henderson

> James Henderson is a pupil in a secondary school in Edinburgh and he is following the GLAFLL* scheme of study in French. This scheme involves working on an individualised programme towards the achievement of clearly stated communicative objectives which are grouped together in graded blocks. Examples of those objectives might be as follows:
>
> Can you:
> – ask the way to well-known places?
> – ask for simple food and drink in a shop?
> (*Waystage 1*)
>
> As James masters each of the objectives he ticks the Pupil column in his Waystage Test Card and either immediately or later he can ask his teacher to test him on the objectives; if he is successful, the teacher ticks the Teacher column (see the example in Appendix D(I)).
>
> When James is ready he can take the appropriate Stage Test, which requires him to apply his knowledge of the foreign language to 'real world' situations. These Stage Tests are proficiency tests and add up to a certification of his competence in French.

This self-assessment is conducted by young people between 12 and 16. In the Waystage Tests, the learners are invited to assess their own mastery of the particular objectives, and then have their assessment confirmed by the teacher. In this way, each pupil decides when she is ready for the test, and she takes the test only to pass it. The pupil also decides when to take the Stage Tests – the proficiency tests.

The approach used by GLAFLL was adapted by Jackson (1980) for use with older learners concerned with more pressing objectives. In these self-rating tests the learner is presented with descriptions of various social and communicative situations and he is asked to:

a) grade himself from 1 to 10 for his ability to handle each situation;
b) get a fellow student to check on his ability and to make a grading on the same scale;
c) get the tutor to grade him on each situation.

* GLAFLL: Graded Levels of Achievement in Foreign Language Learning. See Clark (1980).

This is illustrated by example 7, and an extract from the test is given in Appendix D(I).

Example 7 Mohamed Ali

> Mohamed Ali is studying English in Britain and he is at a pre-intermediate level. He has many needs for English, but the most pressing at this early stage is the language he needs for coping with living in Britain. This includes the obvious vocabulary and simple functions, and a less obvious and less simple understanding of appropriacy in English, and its relation with the expression and perception of particular attitudes and moods. The institution at which Mohamed Ali is studying provides a taught course in 'survival' English, but recognising the importance of the wider context – streets, landlords, shops etc. – as a source of learning, he is given a self-assessment sheet which serves both the function of a test and as a check-list of items to be mastered, so helping to structure his learning outside class.
>
> The items on the sheet range from such things as 'Can you ask a stranger the time?' to 'How would you ask a neighbour to turn down his radio which is disturbing you?'. Mohammed Ali is asked to decide when he can do each of these things (26 items in all), to tick it off on the assessment sheet, and to grade himself 1 to 10 for how well he thinks he can do it. He is then asked to get confirmation of his assessment from certain other people, including the tutor. The results are part of the final assessment.

Diagnostic tests provide information about the learner's strengths and weaknesses in the target language. The most extensive and thorough example of a self-assessment diagnostic test is that produced by von Elek (1982:4). The test covers six skill areas (vocabulary, grammar, listening comprehension, reading comprehension, oral proficiency and written proficiency), and for each there are ten levels of difficulty. The purposes of the tests are broader than just diagnoses, and include helping learners to assume greater responsibility in the evaluation of their proficiency and progress, to diagnose their weak areas and obtain a realistic view of their general proficiency, and to become more motivated and goal-oriented in their further studies. There is a brief illustration of the test in Appendix D(I).

Example 8 Francis Capaldi (II)

> Once the learners were confirmed in their classes (see example 5) the teacher suggested that they co-operated with him on finding out their relative abilities in the various skill areas and in trying to identify the areas of difficulty they had. To do this he suggested

that they use a self-assessment test in Swedish as a second language*.

When Francis Capaldi got the test, he discovered it was much more like a series of exercises than a test; though it was very long, he could do it in his own time and there was none of the stress usually associated with tests and examinations.

The test had ten levels of difficulty for each of six skill areas (vocabulary, grammar, listening comprehension, reading comprehension, oral proficiency and written proficiency), and Francis worked through the difficulty levels until he got stuck. In fact he didn't get very far – especially in grammar, reading comprehension and written proficiency, but he did better in the other areas. The test presented various kinds of problems to the learners and they judged whether or not they could solve them satisfactorily. For example:

a) Can you fill in the gap in this sentence?
– What .... is the dress? It's red.

or b) Could you explain the difference between a restaurant and a café?*

This is also a test designed by someone else, but administered and marked by the learner. It is also possible for the learner to design her own tests (though of course they will be much simpler), but for some learners they may be more focused on relevant learning objectives. The following example illustrates a learner-designed test which is partly for diagnostic purposes and partly designed to give information about progress.

Example 9 Liz Pearson

Liz Pearson, who is learning French to become a bilingual secretary (see Chapter 1), gets help from her French teacher at the French Institute to assess her written French. The teacher has obtained several photocopies of business letters in French concerned with matters similar to those with which Liz Pearson deals daily in her secretarial work in Edinburgh. Liz Pearson uses a selection of the letters to test her growing ability to understand the content and tone, and she then attempts to reply appropriately in French. Liz types the reply and gives it and the original letter to her teacher, who, together with the secretary at the Institute, comments on the appropriateness and the accuracy of the letter. The secretary then gives Liz a copy of the reply she typed originally, and Liz compares this with her version according to a checklist her teacher has given her. (See the description of 'Reformulation' in Appendix C(I).) Liz Pearson, who keeps

* von Elek (1982)

records of her 'scores' (estimated from the number and type of comments), believes she is making steady improvement in writing business letters, though thinks she still has some way to go. She looks forward to the day when she will be able to test her ability to do French audio-typing, that is, typing directly from a recording. The secretary at the Institute has offered to keep cassette recordings of dictated letters and so on, but Liz recognises that she is not ready for that yet.

These examples show *assessment* merging into *practice* and indeed some readers might object that the illustration is a practice technique rather than a test. The answer to that objection relates once again to the question of who requires the information. If the purpose of a progress test is to provide information primarily to the learner then the function of practice and testing can be happily merged. If the purpose is to provide reliable information to others, then more formal techniques will be required.

It is in the areas of *continuous progress testing* and *self-monitoring* that self-assessment has its most obvious place. The purpose of continuous progress testing is to provide information to the learner and teacher on progress within the course; self-monitoring is also concerned with providing information, but only to the learner. This is discussed further below. First, here is an example of self-assessment used for continuous progress testing.

Example 10 Franz Mundt

In one self-access resource centre there are packages of listening materials of various levels of difficulty grouped by subject matter. Franz Mundt has just completed one of these packages, and he is now doing the listening comprehension test which is included in the package. It consists of a cassette and a test form to be filled in whilst listening to the cassette. Franz is free to do the test whenever he wishes – before using the listening package, if he wants to – which gives him more definite information about the suitability of the material, or at any point whilst he is using the package. When he has finished the test Franz will score his responses by referring to the answer sheet which he gets from a file of answer sheets kept separate from the packages. He records the score in his own learner's handbook, which includes a record keeping section. The answer sheet also contains advice on what action to take next. If his score is good-to-high, he is advised to progress to a higher level of material. If it is in the middle band he is advised to do another package at about the same level. If it is low, he is advised to contact a helper, who will investigate further and then may recommend remedial work in listening. Franz can 'cheat' if he wants to; that is, he can get the

> answer sheet before doing the test and adjust his responses to fit those on the answer sheet, or indeed just copy them out from the answer sheet. Since it is his intention to improve his competence in the target language, and since he is not competing with anyone, he feels that there is little point in cheating.

Self-monitoring means self-assessment directed towards action. Thus, in self-monitoring, when the self-assessment shows a deviation or deficiency, this is corrected by the language learner either on the spot, or at some later time. Self-monitoring differs from testing in terms of the degree of privacy of the results of the activity. Self-monitoring may be both a transient and a private activity, whereas the results of self-assessment may be recorded and are therefore marginally less private. The differences between the two, then, are in matters like how public the information is. If the test supplies information to the teacher then it is public to some degree; if it is public then it must be a little more formal than totally private tests. The differences are also to do with the size of the units concerned. Self-monitoring can be concerned with very small units, the pronunciation of a particular word or sentence, the accuracy of a sentence in the written language, and so on.

Many learners develop informal self-assessment devices which they use to monitor their learning progress. These devices include things like estimating the success of an oral communication in terms of the response of an interlocutor, her facial expression and so on (see example 12); making a rough estimate of their level of reading proficiency by attempting to read a newspaper; estimating their level in writing ability by writing business letters and getting others to reformulate them (see example 9); and estimating their level of listening comprehension by viewing video recordings and listening to the radio and audio recordings (see example 13). These and other self-assessment devices are described in Appendix D(I). We can suppose that all learners develop devices of this sort to a greater or lesser degree, but learners can be helped to refine such devices into more efficient ways of making estimates through training.

Another aspect of self-monitoring is keeping records of the results of the self-assessments. Efficient record keeping is a necessary part of self-assessment since it enables learners to make some estimate of their progress over a period of time. A convenient way for the learner to keep records, and indeed of coping with the other useful bits of paper we have discussed in earlier chapters (for example, needs analysis forms, contracts, records of work completed etc.), is to have them all together in a learner's diary – which might simply be a loose leaf folder, or might be a specially printed booklet.

The kind of record learners keep of their own progress can be at various levels of complexity. Younger learners would perhaps only make a simple check-list of the items which they had completed from the course. Older learners might keep records which included ratings on how well they have learned various units, and how enjoyable the learning experience was. The record might also include scores on the various tests which they have undertaken. More detailed suggestions for diaries, and other record keeping procedures, are made in Appendix D(I).

The next three examples illustrate self-monitoring in reading, speaking and listening, using various kinds of learner-designed tests.

Example 11 Dr Cornelius

Dr Cornelius has learned a great deal of Italian in the two years that she has been studying it. You may remember from Chapter 1 that she began studying Italian because she has become very fond of Italy over the past three or four years, taking her children there on camping holidays. She supplemented the four hours a week evening class by reading and listening to everything in Italian she could get. She is now well ahead of the group in the evening class in listening and reading, but she continues in the class to improve all the other aspects of the language – in particular, the grammatical structure, functions and pronunciation. Being a methodical person she tests herself regularly – about every month – on her reading. She produces a cloze test by photocopying an article in a newspaper (actually she always uses a column produced weekly by the same columnist), blacking out every seventh word, and then, after a lapse of a couple of days, trying to replace the words. She checks her responses against the original newspaper column. She keeps a simple record of her percentage score, and is gratified to see a steady increase over the past year.

Example 12 Adrian Chapman

Adrian Chapman has also made good progress over the two years in which he has been studying French (see Chapter 1). He has continued as an autonomous learner, following a BBC course and supplementing it with other materials from the Learning by Appointment Scheme. He has also continued to use native speaker informants whom he finds through a Learning Exchange Scheme. He tries to meet his informant weekly, and every six weeks or so he organises a test for himself. He chooses a particular topic (the last one was concerned with opening a bank account and cashing cheques because he had just met a new informant who had recently come to the UK to study and she actually wanted to know about the subject). Then he learns the appropriate vocabulary, and if he can find suitable books, he learns particular phrases and expressions. When he is ready, he gives an account of the topic to the informant. Adrian has a fairly rough and ready way of assessing himself, but he reckons that it works quite well. He keeps a check on such 'body language' signals as frowning, shrugging, eye glazing, yawning, and so on, as well as the number of repetitions, and rephrasings signalled as needed by the listener, and comes up with an A to E grade. He also asks his informant for some kind of grading, but these grades he finds less useful. Since his informants are mostly students, they change fairly often. Also they tend to give high values to aspects of accuracy in pronunciation and grammar and to devalue communicative effectiveness which is what Adrian is actually after. He also keeps records, but doesn't think they are of much use since there are so many variables affecting his performance at any time – difficulty of the subject, perceptiveness of the listener, his own enthusiasm, and so on. However, it is his distinct impression that the exercise is getting easier, which, as he says, must indicate something!

Example 13 Mary Shields

Another way of self-testing comprehension of the spoken language is that used by Mary Shields, an intermediate learner of French. She makes video recordings of all French language films shown on television. She views the film, using the sub-titles when necessary to supplement her comprehension or to check her guesses, and then after a time lapse of a week or so she tests herself. She selects a two-minute segment, usually at random, covers up the bottom of the screen to mask the sub-titles, and then plays the clip in ten- or twenty-second bursts. She writes rough translations of the dialogue, replays and checks them against the sub-titles. (Often she doesn't trouble to write down the translations for such short segments.) She does not keep records, but a more methodical person might do so.

The final example is from a beginner in the target language, and illustrates the way learners can use the text book for self-assessment.

Example 14 Maura Owen

Maura Owen is studying German at evening classes. She started six months ago, as a complete beginner, and though she does the homework set by the teacher regularly, she doesn't have the time or energy to supplement her study with other materials. The course book does not have review lessons, nor does it have tests built into it; nor does the teacher give regular tests or reviews. Consequently Maura arranges her own. When the evening class has completed a 'unit' of five lessons or so Maura spends two or three hours giving herself a rudimentary attainment test. She chooses one or two written exercises from each of the past five lessons of the book, and does them without reference to the explanations and examples in the course book. She then checks her answers by referring to the explanations and examples. If she is uncertain, she consults a friend who is a competent speaker of German. It would be simpler, she feels, if the course book had answers to the exercises and problems but she suspects that she learns more by finding out the answers for herself. Her German-speaking friend also helps her with the oral exercises in the course book. Maura selects one oral exercise from each of the past five lessons, and she asks her friend to check her pronunciation and grammatical correctness. Maura doesn't record the scores she gets, but she does take careful note of things she has forgotten or things she still finds difficult and she tries to do some extra work on them.

8.3 The feasibility of self-assessment

We have already considered an aspect of the feasibility of self-assessment in the early part of this chapter when we argued that self-assessment was less appropriate for summative testing purposes, that is, collecting information for reporting to a third person as the basis for making decisions about the learner, than for formative purposes. But whatever the purpose of the assessment many readers will want to know what degree of content validity learner-constructed tests are likely to have, and how closely results from self-assessments compare with other, more traditional measurements like teacher-conducted tests and teachers' reports on learners.

If learner-constructed tests are closely related to the learning material used – the course book, for example – then the content validity may be protected to some extent. Also, where the test samples the actual language behaviour aimed at, such as the learner's ability to write a business letter in the target language, or her ability to read part of a newspaper, then once again the content validity is likely to be reasonable. However, there is no doubt that most learners will not be skilled test constructors and some of their self-testing will go amiss. Mary Shields (see example 13) may choose a particularly difficult segment of a video recording, or Liz Pearson may attempt to reply to a particularly tricky business letter (see example 9). But so long as the learners recognise that this will sometimes happen, and so long as the self-testing is a relatively continuous process, these difficulties do not matter very much.

8.3.1 Self-assessment compared to conventional testing

The comparison of self-assessment with conventional testing comes down to two questions:

- Can learners make reasonable assessments of their own learning?
- Will they make accurate assessments?

There are some indications in research results that learners can make satisfactorily accurate self-assessments. There have in recent years been three useful surveys of research in self-assessment, Oskarsson (1978), Heidt (1979) and Oskarsson (1984); the two surveys conducted by Oskarsson relate specifically to self-assessment in language learning, whilst that by Heidt is concerned with education in general.

The general conclusion reached by Oskarsson (1984) is that there is a fairly consistent overall agreement between self-assessment and external criteria. This is encouraging, but we must be cautious about using it to justify self-assessment as it is interpreted in this book. All of the studies which Oskarsson examines use rating scales which have been designed by a tester or the teacher, and completed by the learner. (See examples of self-rating scales in Appendix D(I).) It would clearly be wrong to conclude from Oskarsson's findings that all the forms of self-assessment described here – including those in which the learner herself designs the test – would yield equally satisfactory results.

Assuming that learners *can* make reasonable self-estimates, the question being asked here is 'Will they?' Or to put the question more directly, can learners be trusted to be honest in their self-assessments, or will they succumb to the temptation to cheat?

Firstly, one must distinguish between the natural tendency of learners to interpret doubtful or ambiguous results in their own favour, and the deliberate falsification of results. It is probably inevitable that most learners assessing themselves will be biased in their own favour, which will result in a certain distortion of test results. However this does not seem to be serious judging from Oskarsson's report.

Will learners cheat when they are assessing themselves? We do not know, but it is worth pursuing this issue a little further. 'Cheating' is a process in which a learner seeks to obtain personal advantage – a higher mark or a higher place in the ranking – by unfair means. Cheating, then, is not about learning but about demonstrating the results of learning to someone else. When it is the demonstration of the results of learning which is favoured above the learning itself, then cheating is a real possibility. When it is the achievement of particular objectives which is important to an individual and when it is the learner herself who is most interested in whether the objectives have been achieved or not, then cheating becomes pointless. Children cheat partly because they are encouraged to do so by a system which values scores and rank orders over actual success in learning. Indeed often the system interprets success in learning in terms of these things alone. Where the learner is concerned with real learning objectives, and where self-assessment is mainly used, cheating offers no advantages. It is to counteract this emphasis on 'product', which results in part from a highly teacher-centred approach to education, that greater self-direction is being recommended in this book.

8.4 Conclusion

This chapter has argued that self-assessment used for formative purposes is both possible and desirable. It is most appropriate as the assessment purposes approach self-monitoring, but it is feasible for other assessment purposes, including testing for placement and diagnostic testing. Self-assessment is desirable since it is essential for a learner preparing for autonomy to be able to make some kind of judgement about the accuracy and appropriacy of her performance, and also because self-assessment emphasises learning, the process, rather than the results, the product.

Conclusion

This book has been concerned with attitudes to language learning and how to change them. Throughout the book an attempt has been made to take seriously the proposition that it is the learner who must be responsible for his own learning. The justifications for such a view were explored in Part I, and the remainder of the book has been concerned with exploring the implications of this view in terms of learning materials, resources and their organisation, the supplying of structure, and the preparation of people.

Several important issues have been identified as essential, or at least important, in the implementation of a self-instructional learning mode. First, the examination of what might be meant by self-instruction in Chapter 1 established an important distinction between materials-centred self-instruction – a learning mode which exerts control over the learner through the materials and so severely curtails his freedom – and learner-centred self-instruction – a learning mode in which the learner controls his own learning.

A second set of issues were discussed around the theme of justifications for self-instruction in Chapter 2. These include the well-known arguments for self-instruction concerned with the opening of learning opportunities to those whose access has been limited through such things as job and family responsibilities, geographical constraints and so on. However, self-instruction was also justified through less obvious – and perhaps less concrete – arguments. Thus self-instruction with its consequent greater flexibility of materials and techniques will possibly go further towards accommodating individual differences among learners. Changes in role relations between learners and tutor, and among the learners themselves, may help to reduce certain of the affective barriers to learning, and so promote motivation. By the nature of self-instruction, learners must discover a great deal about how to learn a language, and this training is useful for future language learning. Finally the development of autonomy (both learning and personal autonomy) is an important goal in education which is facilitated through self-instruction.

Two issues which occupied much of the middle of the book are those concerned with learning purpose and learning structure. The major difference in practical implementation between conventional teacher-directed learning and self-instruction is the means of providing purpose and structure to the learner. In the former mode these are supplied largely by or through the teacher. Purpose, in terms of goals and short term objectives, is supplied ultimately by the syllabus or the examination, but it is shaped by the teacher into lesson-sized units, so that learners know through the teacher what their objectives are for this lesson, for this week, and perhaps for the term. Within a self-instructional mode means have to be developed for helping learners to identify their goals and for breaking these down into objectives. Similarly, means have to be found for supplying a structure for the achievement of these objectives, so providing guidance about when they should be tackled, how intensively, in what order, through which medium and so on. These particular questions were addressed in Chapter 5 where devices such as needs analysis questionnaires and learner contracts were discussed.

Another matter concerned both with purpose and structure is learning materials. The two main issues discussed in Chapter 4 are the specific design criteria necessary for self-instructional materials, and how to go about adapting existing materials to meet those criteria more closely.

A fourth major issue related to purpose and structure is the means available to the learner for discovering whether the objectives he set himself have been achieved, that is, ways of assessing himself. The extensive discussion of self-assessment in Chapter 8 concluded, not surprisingly, that in so far as the assessment purpose was in general formative, then self-assessment was a possibility, but that summative assessment was the responsibility of the institution.

The final, essential, component of self-instruction is the preparation of both teachers and learners. Teachers may require psychological preparation to help them adjust to the new and very demanding change of roles in self-instruction. Learners require both psychological and methodological preparation, the first to change attitudes and the second to provide them with the necessary practical expertise in handling contracts, using materials, and undertaking self-assessment. It was also suggested in Chapter 7 that a programme to heighten language awareness and a programme of training in learning strategies would be beneficial in language learning whatever instructional mode is used.

Let me make two points in conclusion. The first is to stress that the approach taken to the introduction of self-instruction in this book is *gradualist* (where this is possible), so that learners are introduced to self-instruction bit by bit, and they always have the opportunity of reverting to a conventional mode, if their circumstances so allow. The second point is that any discussion of self-instruction is to a large extent a discussion about language learning in general and so, whatever you ultimately think about self-instruction, there are, I believe, many questions discussed here of relevance to all language teachers and all language learners.

Appendices

Appendix A Preparation in the completion of contracts

As we said in Chapter 5, learners need quite a lot of help with completing contracts when they are first introduced. It is worthwhile spending some time on this, not only because it helps to make contract learning run smoothly, but also because it gets learners thinking about objectives and assessment, and, for learners beyond the beginning stages, gives good practice in meaningful oral communication.

The first stage in preparation is to introduce the contract gradually, as suggested in Chapter 5. Learners are thus asked to make decisions about small segments of their learning – for example decisions about what extensive reading to do over the next week or decisions about what material to use during a self-study period. Several of the systems illustrated in Chapter 3 asked the learner to make choices from among a number of options – the Circle Model and the Private Study Model for example. The Flower Model requires the learners to make more extensive choices once they are operating the full system, but there is a lengthy period of preparation before they are asked to do this. The next stage of preparation for contract learning is to introduce the full contract to the learners. The first stage of this could be to distribute a contract which has already been completed and get the learners to evaluate it. The purposes of this are to get learners thinking about objectives, and especially to get them to distinguish between clear and achievable objectives and vague and unrealistic ones; to get them thinking about appropriate materials and activities for meeting objectives, and about suitable means of self-assessment. These are all difficult matters and the scheme suggested below may have to be repeated on a number of occasions with different examples.

Evaluating a completed contract

- The teacher distributes copies of the completed contract and explains the meaning of the column headings on the contract form. This can be

done using the information in Chapter 6, illustrated by the examples in the completed contract.
– The class divides into groups of three and the teacher distributes the set of evaluation questions suggested below. Groups spend about twenty minutes evaluating the example contract. The groups then report their findings in a plenary session.

Evaluation questions

Learning objectives

– Are the objectives clear and understandable?
– Do they describe what the individual is setting out to *learn* (rather than what he plans to *do*)?
– Is each objective stated in such a way that the learner can know when it has been achieved?
– Are they limited and so achievable within a week or two (i.e. the time span of the contract)?
– Are there sufficient/too many objectives for the time available?

Proposed activities (what the learner is going to do)

– Are the proposed activities relevant to the achievement of the objective?
– Are the activities feasible, given the time and resources available?
– Are there other activities that could be used?

Proposed resources (what the learner is going to use)

– Are the resources relevant for undertaking the proposed activities?
– Are there other resources, particularly human resources, that could be helpful?
– Has the learner considered using relevant authentic documents for practising the activities?
– Are the resources easily available at times the learner wants them?
– Is it desirable and possible to organise a group of learners to work on this/these objectives?

Ways of demonstrating the achievement of the objectives

– Is the self-assessment technique proposed clearly relevant to the objective and the activities used?
– Are there tests available in the materials being used?

- Are there relevant tests available elsewhere?
- Are the criteria proposed clear, relevant and able to be applied?
- Is the self-assessment technique convincing to other members of the group?
- Is there a way of using a peer (or a group of peers) to help with the assessment?

Completion of individual contracts

Objectives

- Each learner completes a learner contract, specifying which objectives are considered relevant.
- Learners are given further practice in evaluating contracts.

Procedure

- Individuals complete a contract form (with two carbon copies) covering a short period of learning. (This will depend on the amount of time the learners have available, but roughly around six hours of actual study time.) They are free to confer with other members of their group of three, and if they wish the group can complete the contracts co-operatively. The teacher and any other helpers available circulate in the room, consulting wherever there is a need.
- Each individual's contract is examined by the other two members of the group, and they spend up to about twenty minutes giving feedback to each individual. Once again, the set of evaluation questions provides a useful framework. If groups completed the contract co-operatively, it may be more profitable to form fresh groups for this evaluation procedure.

Materials

- Blank contract forms
- Carbon paper
- List of evaluation questions (see above)

Appendix B Preparation of teachers

We said in Chapter 7 that some teachers may benefit from preparation in self-instruction, especially those who are new to this mode, who lack confidence in themselves to help learners in self-instruction, and those who are doubtful or sceptical about self-instruction. The suggestions for preparation which follow are not primarily intended to persuade teachers to adopt a self-instructional mode, rather the intention is to give them the opportunity of discovering what is meant by self-instruction in the whole range of its meanings, and also to allow them to explore their feelings about it. The first section is concerned with aspects of psychological preparation and the second with methodological preparation.

Psychological preparation

What is self-instruction?

This is an activity designed to help people to find out about self-instruction.

Objectives

- To discover what is meant by self-instruction;
- To consider what type and degree of self-instruction would be appropriate for a described set of learners in some particular situation.

Resources

- Chapters 1, 3 and 7 of this book.
- Gross (1979) Chapter 2, pp. 23–48.
- Tough (1979) Chapter 3, pp. 16–32.

Tasks

- Participants are asked to produce a definition or a brief description of self-instruction. They are asked to read the references beforehand, though it is useful if these can also be available during the activities session. Individuals attempt to formulate a definition or description and then agree on a common formulation with another person. It may be possible to sustain this to group level – two or three pairs agreeing a definition or description.

  The main value of this activity is the discussion that goes on while attempting to come to an agreement.
- Using a similar procedure, participants are asked to produce an agreed list of points for and against self-instruction. The various reports can be discussed at a plenary session.

- Participants are asked to make specific proposals (though in outline) for elements of self-instruction suitable for a specified set of learners following a particular course.
- In addition to these activities, some of those suggested for the psychological preparation of learners could also be used with teachers.

The characteristics of the ideal helper

This is concerned with changes of role expected of teachers operating in a self-instructional mode.

Objectives

- To enable participants to reflect on the changing role of the teacher in a self-instructional mode;
- To consider in detail what the role of the helper is;
- To list the personal characteristics necessary to fulfil this role.

Resources

- The list of the characteristics of the ideal helper in Chapter 7 of this book.
- Tough (1979) pp. 177–84.
- Rogers (1969) Chapter 7, pp. 164–6.
- Rogers (1969) Chapter 4.

Task

Draw up a list of the characteristics and skills of the ideal helper for the learning situation *in your institution.*

Self-assessment

The following activities are all directly concerned with various changes of role that teachers need to adjust to in a self-instructional mode. Many, of course, will find these role changes easy, indeed they may already relate to learners in ways facilitative of self-instruction. Others may find it difficult to change their attitudes to learners and to learning activities. Preparation for learners' self-assessment is concerned first with possible attitudes of teachers towards self-assessment, and then with aspects of the teacher's role in preparing learners for self-assessment. Attitudes to assessment are crucially important to self-instruction. The success of a learner-centred approach to self-instruction is dependent upon the learner being willing and able to take on responsibility for his own learning; and this is often dependent upon the teacher being willing to share this responsibility. The teacher's willingness to relinquish sole responsibility for grading and assessment could be a big issue in the success of a self-instructional programme.

Objectives

- To enable participants to reflect upon their attitudes to assessment, with particular reference to the respective roles of teacher and learner;
- To consider the feasibility of self-assessment;
- To consider the desirability of emphasising formative assessment at the expense of summative assessment.

Resources

- Heron (1981) especially pp. 57–61.
- Pirsig (1974) Chapter 16, especially pp. 190–6.
- Tough (1979) pp. 158–63.
- Rogers (1969) Chapter 6, pp. 151–5.
- Chapter 8 of this book.

Tasks

- Participants are asked to respond to Carl Rogers' conclusions about grades and examinations:

  ... by themselves these interpretations of my experience may sound queer and aberrant, but not particularly shocking. It is when I realize the implications that I shudder a bit at the distance I have come from the commonsense world that everyone knows is right ...
  - Such experience would imply that we would do away with teaching. People would get together if they wished to learn.
  - We would do away with examinations. They measure only the inconsequential type of learning.
  - We would do away with grades and credits for the same reason.
  - We would do away with degrees as a measure of competence partly for the same reason. Another reason is that a degree marks an end or a conclusion of something, and a learner is only interested in the continuing process of learning.
  - We would do away with the exposition of conclusions, for we would realize that no one learns significantly from conclusions.

- Participants are asked to consider the two questions posed in Chapter 8 of this book:
  - Can learners make reasonably accurate self-assessments?
  - Will learners make reasonably accurate self-assessments?

Helping learners in self-assessment

The second aspect of self-assessment concerns the kinds of things teachers may be involved in when they are helping learners.

Resources

- Chapter 8 of this book.
- Oskarsson (1984).
- Windeatt (1981).

Tasks

- Specify a number of language learning goals – for example, developing fluency in spontaneous spoken language – and devise ways that learners can self-assess their achievement.
- Consider critically one of the examples of self-assessment tests in Chapter 8 and Appendix D(I) of this book. Make suggestions for modification.

Methodological preparation

The workshops suggested here are all concerned with examples of tasks which teachers may be asked to undertake when they are helping in a self-instructional mode.

Needs analysis

Resources

- Chapter 5 of this book.
- Allwright (1982) pp. 24–31.
- Munby (1978) Chapter 10.

Tasks

- Examine a needs analysis questionnaire and modify it to suit your situation.
- Design a needs analysis questionnaire to be used by learners.
- Design an interview schedule to be used by a tutor to elicit learners' needs.

Materials evaluation, adaptation and preparation

Resources

- Chapter 4 of this book.
- Geddes and Sturtridge (1982).
- Cross (1980).
- Logan (1980).
- Windeatt (1981).

Tasks

- Construct a text book evaluation schedule from the criteria in Chapter 4, and apply it to a course book.
- Apply the text book evaluation schedule to a course book, identify needs for adaption to make the book more suitable for self-instruction, and adapt it.
- Produce a unit of self-instructional materials for a specified group of learners. Carefully record the problems met in preparing the materials and the proposed solutions.

Setting up a self-access resource

Resources

- Chapter 6 of this book.
- Riley and Zoppis (1976).
- Geddes and Sturtridge (1982).
- Harding-Esch (1982).

Tasks

- Produce a specification of the components of a self-access resource in the ideal system.
- Propose a plan for the development of a self-access resource over a period of, say, four years.

The training of learners for self-instruction

Resources

- Stanchina and Riley (1978).

Tasks

- Take a course book and consider what training learners would need to use it in a self-instructional mode.
- What particular learning activities could you suggest to autonomous groups?
- What uses can learners make of their own authentic documents? What training would they need?

Specific training for language learning

Resources

- Chapter 7 of this book.

- Cohen and Aphek (1981).
- Rubin (1981).
- Wesche (1979).

Tasks

- Participants, individually and then in pairs, recall their own language learning experience and confirm and add to the list of learning strategies in Chapter 7.
- Sort the strategies into those that can be usefully taught and those that cannot.
- Consider how to train learners in these strategies. Each group takes one strategy and proposes a way of training learners in it.
- Consider how these strategies could be introduced into the language learning programme.

Conducting workshops

Gibbs (1981:93) suggests a way of organising workshops – he calls them Structured Group Exercises – which involves participants first thinking through a problem individually, then working in pairs, sharing with one other person the results of their thinking; then two or three pairs join together to form small groups within which the decisions reached by each pair are formulated into a group response to the topic. Finally, there is a plenary session, chaired by the tutor, at which each group reports its results. This structure is a very effective way of involving everyone in a group in a discussion, since it gives everyone the opportunity to express their opinions, anxieties and so on under the least threatening conditions. It also emphasises co-operative learning.

Appendix C(I) Techniques for psychological and methodological preparation of learners

The techniques described below would ideally be used with *groups* of learners, but under some circumstances it may be necessary to adapt them to single individuals.

Appendix C(I)

Psychological preparation

The following suggestions are concerned with demonstrating to learners what self-instruction is, and that it is a viable learning mode.

Describing self-instruction

Resources

– Chapters 1 and 8 of this book.

Activity

This might begin with a general description of the possibilities – using a device similar to Figure 2 in Chapter 1 – and then give several examples similar to those in Chapter 1. This could be extended into describing self-assessment, using a similar approach – a description of the possibilities, and several relevant examples.

For and against

Objectives

– To express anxieties about, and aspirations for a self-instructional learning mode;
– To consider one's own and others' anxieties and aspirations carefully.

Resources

– Gross (1979) pp. 17 and 18.
– Rogers (1969) Chapter 6, pp. 152–5.

Activity

Following the tutor's introduction to self-instruction, individuals list points in favour of and against self-instruction. Pairs combine their lists and then groups attempt to agree on, say, three major points for self-instruction and three against. The following plenary session is concerned first with establishing a total list of points and, secondly, and most importantly, with discussing them.

Learning project I

Objective

– To show that self-instruction is a viable learning mode.

Resources

- Tough (1979) Chapter 3, pp. 16–32, in particular the quantitative findings of his research.
- Gross (1979) Chapter 2, pp. 23–48, in particular the examples he gives of learners and their projects.
- Chapters 1 and 8 of this book.

Activity

The tutor reviews Tough's quantitative data on adult learning projects, and gives examples from Gross, and this book. Participants individually note two or three learning projects they have undertaken over the past year and also note any particular difficulties or satisfaction they found with them. Pairs put two lists together and consider the difficulties to see if they can find a solution. Groups operate likewise.

Learning project II

Objective

- To demonstrate that self-instruction is a viable language learning mode.

Resources

- Whatever is relevant to the tasks selected.

Activity

Participants are helped to select a relevant limited language learning objective. This is easier if this activity follows needs analysis for those learners to whom it is relevant. However, the objective should be achievable within an hour or two of learning time. Examples of this might include discovering a satisfactory explanation for some grammatical point, or discovering the expressions of some communicative function in the target language, such as appropriate ways of expressing thanks to the hostess after a dinner party or polite expressions to use when asking where the lavatory is.

Participants begin working on their objective(s) during a class session where they can be helped to plan the work, decide what resources, material or human, would be useful in helping to achieve it, discover how to obtain these resources, and decide how to assess whether, and to what degree, they have achieved their objective(s).

In some circumstances it will be necessary for participants to work on these objectives in their own time, outside of a classroom session; in others it will be possible for participants to work on them in class where the teacher is available to give assistance. Anyway, participants work on their chosen objectives and try to achieve them. They are asked to note any particularly successful techniques they use, and whatever difficulties they encounter.

Finally students, working in pairs and then in groups, make a simple collation of successful techniques and particular difficulties, after which they seek solutions for the difficulties. The plenary session following should focus on the solutions of problems, and these solutions can be added to the list of techniques.

Methodological preparation

Methodological preparation is concerned with preparing learners to undertake the actual tasks of language learning in a self-instructional mode. The majority of suggestions which follow are concerned with the use of authentic texts.

Choosing authentic documents to study

Learners need guidance on selecting listening and reading texts as well as preparation in how to use them. When the document is a written text it may be necessary simply to have regard to topic and length, and maybe to an estimate of linguistic complexity measured perhaps by sentence length or some more precise index of readability. The selection of a recording of spoken language would consider many more criteria. This list from Riley (1981) might function both as a useful guide to the cataloguing of a listening resource, and as a check-list to be suggested to learners to take into account when selecting a text.

- *Topic.* What is the recording about?
- *Setting.* What is the physical context of the recording (for example a conference, a radio talk, etc.)?
- *Number of speakers.* Is it a monologue (only one speaker), a dialogue (two speakers), or are there more than two speakers?
- *Clarity.* What is the level of background noise, traffic noise, other speakers, etc., which might make the recording more difficult to understand?
- *Spontaneous or prepared.* Is the text read from a prepared script either as a monologue or acted in a dialogue, or is it spontaneous?
- *Formal or informal.* What is the degree of formality/informality of the language?
- *Accents.* Do all the speakers use a standard accent familiar to the listener or do some use regional accents likely to be unfamiliar?
- *Speed of delivery.* How fast is the delivery? A BBC newsreader running short of time can read the news at a surprisingly fast rate.

– *Length.* How long is the recording?
– *Date of production.* How current is the information?
– *Supporting materials.* Is there a transcription available? Are there any other supporting materials?

Study techniques

The following suggestions to learners for study techniques are taken largely from three sources, Moulden (1982), Riley (1981) and Dickinson (1980). These suggestions do not take account of the learners' levels. Some may be appropriate only for intermediate to advanced learners.

Work on written texts

The majority of the suggestions here come from Moulden (1982:25).

– *Reading speed.* Time yourself while reading a text. Global comprehension can be checked by reading the text again carefully. Reading-speed tables can be found in several places – for example, de Leeuw (1965).
– *Search reading.* Use the title, illustrations and perhaps the introduction to generate questions on the content of the text. Try to answer the questions quickly by reading the text. Be prepared to revise the questions as you read. Check the answers by reading the text more carefully. Get another learner to read the text, and discuss your questions and answers with the other person. Finally, if all else fails to solve a problem, ask a teacher/counsellor or find someone with a competent knowledge of the language.
– *Reading comprehension.* Work with another learner. Each take a different text or a different part of the same text. Read it carefully and prepare questions for the other person. Exchange texts and answer the other person's questions. Discuss the answers you have each given to the other person's questions. Use texts for which there is a translation to check on global and detailed comprehension.

Many of these ideas can be put together in ways such as those suggested in the 'Standard Reading Exercise' suggested by Scott *et al.* (1984). They suggest that tutors construct a standard exercise which can be used on any text. The questions are written in the learners' mother tongue. The form of the standard exercise which they use is reproduced in Appendix C(II).

Texts as the basis for grammar, vocabulary and discourse exercises and problem solving. Work either with a partner or alone. If you work alone, you will have to allow a lapse of time between preparing the activity and actually doing it.

- *Cloze tests and exercises.* Select a text and make a photocopy. Prepare a cloze test either by blocking out every seventh word, or by blocking out selected word types – for example, verb forms, or prepositions or articles. Your partner (or you, after a time lapse) replaces the missing words. Check the answers on the original. If you are working on your own, cut a narrow strip of paper and place it across a reading text (you will probably need to fold it or you will see through it!). Read the text and attempt to replace the obscured words, part words and phrases. You can alter the level of difficulty by changing the width of the strip (Riley 1980).
- *Mechanical exercises.* Many of the exercise types used in (older) course books can be prepared almost automatically, though this sometimes results in very difficult activities. For example, one learner writes out the sentences of a paragraph at random, the other rearranges. Parts of sentences can be obliterated on a copy of a text by one learner, the other attempts to reconstruct them. Other examples include changing all the verbs in a set of sentences to another tense and making other necessary changes. Change the number to plural/singular and make the necessary changes. Change the gender of the subject; change from affirmative to negative, etc.

Work on recorded texts

- *Global comprehension.* Listen to the recording and try to get a general idea of what it is about. Check comprehension by listening more carefully, stopping and replaying sections and/or by using a transcription* of the recording, and check it against the transcription supplied.
- *'Heighten' the transcription you have made.* That is, convert it into an acceptable written form of the language by removing all the false starts, hesitation phenomena, repetitions and so on, and put it into the normal sentence organisation of the written language.
- *Selective listening.* Construct questions from the title of the talk and from the introduction. Listen to the recording for the answers, revising the questions as you proceed. Check the answers by reading the transcript.
- *Work with another learner.* Each construct comprehension questions on a different recording (or a different part of the same one). Exchange questions, and answer them. Discuss questions and answers with your partner. Check answers against the transcript.
- *Summary writing.* Take notes from the recording as you listen. Write

* Transcribe and transcription here refer to a version written out in standard orthography – not in phonetic symbols.

a summary from the notes. Check the summary either against the original recording or/and against a transcription.

A 'Standard Listening Exercise' can be constructed on the model of the Standard Reading Exercise. (See the example in Appendix C(III).)

Practice in specific listening skills

- *Memory (I).* Stop the cassette and repeat the last few words. Rewind and check.
- *Memory (II).* Stop the cassette and try to remember the last two or three points the speaker has made. Rewind and check.
- *Prediction.* As you listen, try to predict what the speaker will say. This can be either prediction of the actual words or prediction of the content.
- *Guessing strategies.* When listening to a new text for the first time, attempt to piece together the sense from the fragments you understand. Check by more careful listening and/or by using the transcription.
- *Pronunciation (I).* Shadow the speaker in a recording, and if you are using a language laboratory compare your version with the original.
- *Pronunciation (II).* Read from a transcript and compare your recording with the original. Clearly, learners will need help and preparation in devising these activities.

Communicative activities

Communicative activities concerned with the written language may be relatively easily initiated by the learner. The work Liz Pearson has undertaken in practising reading business letters and replying to them has already been described (see example 3 Chapter 1). Advanced language learners who are involved in scientific research in a medium other than their mother tongue frequently need to write papers or a dissertation and learn on the job, as it were, by getting someone to read and criticise what they have written.

In addition, post-intermediate learners can benefit from an activity described by Cohen (1983), which he calls 'reformulation'. After writing two or more drafts of the essay, and getting feedback from peers and teachers on the writing, the writer gets a native speaker of the target language (or failing a native speaker, a competent non-native) to reformulate part or all of the essay in his own words making it read in a 'native-like' way. There are no constraints put on the reformulator; he uses whatever vocabulary and style he thinks is appropriate. The learner then compares the two versions, either with the reformulator or alone. Cohen recommends that the comparison is made along the following lines:

- *Lexis.* Vocabulary is compared word for word.
- *Syntax.* The text is examined for word order and the choice and ordering of clauses.
- *Cohesion.* The text is examined for differences in pronominal reference, use of conjunctions and lexical substitution.
- *Discourse functions.* The marking of discourse functions are compared.
- *Paragraphs.* Physical and conceptual paragraphs are compared.

The specific problems *vis-à-vis* the target language of learners with particular mother tongues can be emphasised in the comparison.

Some learners with highly specialist requirements in communication in the spoken language may also initiate simulated activities. Stanchina and Riley (1978) describe the case of Dr A, a French cardiologist who wished to attend a conference held in English where he would give a slide lecture and act as chairman of one of the round table discussions. As part of his language preparation for these events, he worked with a helper in simulations of these activities.

In general, however, it would be unrealistic to expect learners to design their own spoken language communication activities, though it may be reasonable to expect them to *manage* such activities themselves after a period of preparation. In order to facilitate this it is necessary to have a large selection of activities available, with simple and clear descriptions of what is to be done. Ideas for activities can be taken from course books and articles (see, for example, Hendrickson 1980, 1983). Games and role-play activities can also be used, providing the instructions of what to do and how to do it are simple and clear (maybe in the learner's mother tongue if this is feasible). Alternative arrangements which preserve the learners' freedom of choice include 'activity options' (Roberts 1975, Geddes and McAlpin 1978) and 'sign-up' options. In activity options a regular time-span is allocated each week from the course timetable, during which learners can choose among several activities. The activities described by Geddes and McAlpin include Games, Listening, Research and Films; they are set up in separate areas and learners can circulate from one to the other. The system of 'sign-up' options has been in use in SCEO for some years. Learners sign up for role-play or simulation activities which are organised by a tutor.

Appendix C(II) The Standard Reading Exercise (Scott *et al.* 1984)

The following is presented in the learners' mother tongue.

1 Read only the title of your text. Predict and write down at least five vocabulary items – key words – which you expect to see in the text. The key words can be noted down in English or in your mother tongue – (Portuguese in the case of Scott's student).
2 Skim the text quickly (maximum one minute), looking for key words in the text. Use all the typographical indications, your previous knowledge, cognates and repeated words. Now write down, in no more than fifteen words, the main theme of the text.

Reread the text as often as necessary to answer the following questions:

1 What seems to be the author's main intention: to persuade you or just to inform you?
2 Write down any words which look important in the text (key words) which you did not know before reading it. Beside each one write down what it probably means.
3 Write down the main idea of each paragraph, using only one sentence for each main idea. If the text consists of more than seven paragraphs, write down the main idea of each section. Avoid translating and try not to mention insignificant ideas.
4 Divide the text into sections. Is there an introduction? If so, where does it end? Is there a conclusion? If so, where does it start? Explain your answer.
5 Write one sentence reporting something which you learned from the text.
6 Critical reaction: whose interests does this text represent? Which country, which social class, which institution? Who would find the publication of this text desirable? Is the information in this text applicable to your own situation?
7 Indicate your interest in this text using a scale from 1 to 5.
8 How many times did you need to use a dictionary to answer the questions so far?
9 Write down the number of each paragraph which you feel you couldn't understand properly, or aren't sure you understood.
10 Try to work out why you found the paragraphs you listed in the last question so difficult. What was the main reason?
   – lack of previous knowledge of the topic
   – a grammatical problem (which one?)
   – inefficient reading strategies
   – difficulty in identifying the introduction or conclusion etc.
11 Now estimate your comprehension of the text (for example, 50 per cent, 80 per cent).

Appendix C(III) The Standard Listening Exercise

The following activity is partly based on Scott *et al.* (1984) – see Appendix C(II). I am also indebted to Moulden (1982) for the analysis of listening problems below.

Identifying listening needs

Let us begin by working out what aspects of your listening skills you might want to improve. First let us consider some things you may wish to *improve* or *learn to do*. Look at this list and see if any of them are relevant to you.

- Listen to lectures and take notes.
- Understand other people's contributions in seminars.
- Understand radio broadcasts.
- Understand television programmes.
- Understand films.
- Understand and take part in conversations.
- Understand conversations which you overhear.
- Listen to and understand English spoken with a particular accent.
- Listen to English of a particular 'formality' level (for example, very formal English or very informal English).
- Listen to English from a particular register (for example, scientific, academic, etc).

You may wish to practise listening with particular purposes.

- Listening for information (for example, telephone messages).
- Listening for gist (for example, news broadcasts).
- Listening for the details of content (for example, a lecture).
- Listening for the attitudes expressed (for example, in conversations or in speeches).
- Listening for agreement or disagreement (for example, in conversations or in seminars).
- Listening for pleasure (for example, listening to plays, stories, poems or songs).

None of these may cover what you want to do. If that is so, write down what you want to do, or ask your tutor for help.
The item you have chosen will help you to select the right **kind** *of text and* **may** *help you to decide on the objectives of your listening exercises.*

Identifying listening problems

You may have one or more of the following listening problems. Tick them off; they will help you to decide on the kinds of materials and exercises you should prepare.

- *Discrimination*: not being able to hear the difference between sounds that are different.
- *Segmentation*: not being able to hear the sounds of the language as sequences of words.
- *Vocabulary*: not knowing the meaning of individual words you hear.
- *Short-term memory*: not being able to remember the last few words you hear long enough for you to guess or work out their meaning.
- *Compensation*: not being able to guess the meanings of words you did not know or could not hear.
- *Grammar*: not understanding meaning expressed through word structure and word order.
- *Figurative language*: not understanding non-literal use of language (for example, metaphors, idiomatic expressions).
- *Communicative value of utterances*: not realising that an utterance means more than, or something different from, what it appears to mean.
- *External references*: not understanding allusions to things which are not explained by the persons you are listening to.
- *Cohesion and coherence*: not being able to follow the thread of meaning from one utterance to another.
- *Discourse organisation*: not being aware of the signals which help to organise the argument in a spoken text.
- *Long-term memory*: not being able to remember what you have heard long enough to grasp it as a whole.
- *Speed*: speech which is too fast for you to keep up with.

The items you have selected from the list above will be the basis of the objectives for your listening exercises.

Selecting a text

On the basis of the decisions you have made above, select an audio tape or a video tape.
(*Note*: Students may need advice on how to go about this. Clearly the relevant advice will depend on the organisation of the resources in the institute the student is working in.)

Some suggestions

- *Catalogue.* There may be a card catalogue of audio tapes. It will give you an idea of what the tapes are about.
- *The subject catalogue.* This and various lists in the Resources Centre may be helpful for finding out what the recordings are about.
- *Listening courses.* Quite a lot of listening courses use authentic materials. You can use the text from a listening course, but prepare your own exercises to meet *your* needs.
- *Record your own text.* Various radio stations broadcast a lot of material which is suitable for listening practice. If you have the equipment (or if a friend has) you could record an appropriate text.
- *Tutor.* Failing all else, ask the tutor. He *may* be able to help you!

Selecting a segment of the text

How long your text is will depend on what your objectives are for the listening materials. However, the segment will usually be quite short – generally not more than *five minutes* at the outside.

In order to select a segment, you will have to listen to the text – or view it – and choose a part which

- is coherent in itself (that is, it has a natural beginning and end, and makes sense when it is taken out of the context of the rest);
- is interesting.

Standard questions for listening practice

For each text you have selected produce answers to the following questions. (They are adapted from Scott *et al.* 1984.)

1 From the title of the text predict and write down at least five vocabulary items – key words – which you expect to hear in the text. Use a dictionary if necessary. Now, listen to the text and see how many of the words or their near equivalents actually occur.
2 Listen once more to the text – as far as possible without stopping – and then write down *in no more than 20 words* the main theme of the text.

Listen to the text as often as necessary to answer the following questions.

1 What seems to be the author's main intention: to *persuade* the listener, to *inform* the listener, or simply to *entertain*?

2 Write down any words in the text which seem important to understanding it, but which you did not know before listening. Beside each one, write down what you think it means *without using a dictionary*.
3 Is it possible to divide the text into sections? Is there an introduction? If so, where does it end? Is there a conclusion? If so, where does it start? Are there any other sections which you can find?
4 Is the speaker arguing a case? If so, note the arguments used.
5 If the speaker is arguing a case, are examples used to illustrate the argument? Write down what the examples are.
6 Write one sentence reporting something you learned from the text.
7 How interesting is this text for you? Indicate your interest by using a scale of 1 to 5 (5 = very interesting, 1 = very boring).
8 Using the transcript (if there is one), write down the number of each section you couldn't understand properly, or you aren't sure you understood.
9 Try to work out why you found the sections listed above difficult to understand. What was the main reason?
   – lack of previous knowledge of the topic
   – a grammatical problem (which one?)
   – difficulty in separating main points from details
   – difficulty in identifying the introduction or conclusion, etc.
10 For each text please give to the tutor:
   – the title of the listening text
   – your answers to the standard questions.

Appendix D(I) Examples of self-assessment techniques

Learner-prepared self-assessment

It is possible for learners to prepare their own tests and use them with others or with themselves after a lapse of time. Here are a few examples. Language tutors and learners will be able to think up more possibilities in the course of learning and tutoring.

Comprehension questions on listening and reading texts

Learners prepare questions, or other activities, on the pattern of published materials. The questions can then be answered by others – or by the learner himself after a lapse of time. Where there are two or three learners of intermediate level or beyond together, the answers to the questions and the questions themselves constitute valuable discussion topics. Problems about answers for groups and for individuals can be taken to the tutor for solution. Obviously, learners will need practice in making up questions. One way of helping learners is to introduce the exercise by getting them to examine one or more examples of listening comprehension materials based on texts at a lower level than the learners are working at, so they can concentrate on the techniques.

Mechanical tests

Tests can be constructed along similar lines to self-made materials suggested in Appendix C(I) and (II).

Self-assessment of composition writing

Compositions, essays and other continuous written material can be self-assessed and assessed by peers in the manner described in Chapter 8 example 4, and expanded in Appendix D(II).

Self-monitoring of spoken drills and exercises

Self-monitoring is the process in which learners individually check their performance against an internal (or an external) model and adjust aspects of it (usually but not necessarily phonological aspects) to move closer to the model. The ability to monitor one's own performance is an essential learning skill and one therefore that every language learner must acquire. Consequently it is very worthwhile spending time helping learners to acquire these skills.

- For pronunciation, ear training exercises perhaps used in conjunction with transcription.
- For pronunciation in terms of sounds (segmental) and in terms of intonation and stress and (to a lesser degree) in terms of structural accuracy, exercises requiring students to identify errors in recordings of learners at a lower level.
- Monitoring the production of peers and finally self-monitoring using recorded speech.

These activities will only be possible if the tutor supplies the learners with definite objectives for attention, especially in the early stages of preparation. Thus, for example, the tutor focuses on two or three phonemes which have been giving trouble.

In a multi-lingual group, monitoring pairs can be made up, to begin with, of people with different mother tongues, since the errors made in the target language by a speaker of one language may be perceived more easily by someone who speaks another language. Later, monitoring pairs can be made from the same language groups.

Self- and peer-monitoring of spoken performance can be done using video recordings of communicative activities. The activity is carried out and then the video viewed, preferably using some kind of monitoring check-list, guiding the viewers to the kinds of things they should be watching for.

In addition, video (or audio) recordings of individuals' performance can be viewed by the individual several weeks later. This helps learners, especially those at more advanced levels, to realise that they are making progress.*

Self-assessment check-lists

Check-lists are tests consisting of a list of tasks or questions which the learner is asked to respond to. Illustrations are given below from von Elek (1982), who uses this format for a diagnostic test, Oskarsson (1980) and Clark (1980).

Von Elek's test is a self-assessment diagnostic test of Swedish as a foreign language. It covers six skill areas (vocabulary, grammar, listening comprehension, reading comprehension, oral proficiency and written proficiency), and for each there are ten levels of difficulty (see figure 31).

Oskarsson (1980) has five types of self-assessment instruments. Type A asks the learner to estimate his level of proficiency in the four skills of *listening*, *speaking*, *reading*, and *writing* on a ten-point scale. For listening, the lowest point is glossed by the equivalent in the learner's mother tongue of the statement 'I do not understand spoken English at all', and the highest point by the statement 'I understand practically everything that is said to me in English'.

Type B similarly uses a ten-point scale with a gloss at each extremity, but it differs from Type A in that the listening, speaking etc. event is contextualised. For speaking the following context is provided: 'Imagine that you meet an English-speaking person who does not know anything about Sweden. He wants to have as much information as possible about Sweden and therefore asks you questions about living conditions, housing, nature, weather, eating habits, leisure, holidays, sport, radio and television, the royal family, celebrities etc.'

Oskarsson's Type C Self-Assessment Form consists of a set of descriptive rating scales in which there are six descriptions in an 11-point scale.

* Holec (1980) and Oskarsson (1984) report examples of these self-assessment techniques used in Eurocentre, Bournemouth.

READING COMPREHENSION

Each of the ten units (L:1–L:10) consists of at least two of the following types of items:

1. Comprehension of definitions:

   Can you supply the missing word?

   In _____ the goal keeper is the only person who is allowed to touch the ball. (5)
   A _____ is a huge reptile. It moves awkwardly on shore but is extremely swift and dangerous in the water. (7)

2. Comprehension of non-contextual sentences:

   Do you understand the sentence?

   Closed on Saturdays. (1)
   There are two exceptions to this rule. (4)
   Due to our well-organised pre- and post-natal care the infant mortality rate is extremely low. (8)

3. Comprehension of coherent texts.

   The number, length and complexity of the texts varied considerably at different levels. Each text was followed by a number of questions concerning words, expressions or context.

ORAL PRODUCTION

Each of the ten units (M:1–M:10) consists of at least three of the following tape-recorded parts.

1. Repetition of sentences.

   Can you repeat the sentence?

   See you tomorrow! (1)
   This is my daughter Maria. She is eleven. (2)
   If someone had told me ten years ago that I would eventually settle down in Sweden I would have taken it as a joke. (9)

2. Answering questions.

   Can you give an intelligible answer to the question?

   How long have you been in Sweden? (2)
   Can you give some reasons why people emigrate? (6)
   What kind of reform would you like to introduce in your country and why? (9)

Figure 31 Extracts from von Elek's test

These descriptions consist of statements describing increasing levels of proficiency. For example, Level 2 (out of 5) for reading is, 'I understand the meaning of simple written instructions about the way, time, place and similar things, and also understand the essential things in simple texts dealing with familiar subjects such as common leisure interests, current affairs and living conditions.' Level 4 is, 'I understand everything or nearly everything written in the language within non-specialist fields. There may be words I do not understand in difficult texts.'

Types D and E are questionnaires designed for self-assessment at the Threshold Level (van Ek 1976). Type D (see figure 32) consists of a series of questions about the learner's ability to ask and tell interlocutors things about common topics.

Appendix 4: Self-assessment form (Type D)

Sample questionnaire for self-assessment at T-Level

[To be translated into the learner's native language]

Instruction: Imagine that you meet an English-speaking person from another country. He does not know anything about you and your country. Indicate your estimated command of the language by putting a cross in the appropriate box (*Yes* or *No*) for each statement.

4. I can tell him what kinds of food and drink I like and don't like. ☐ Yes ☐ No
5. I can tell him about my interests (hobbies, interests in general, etc.). ☐ Yes ☐ No

14. I can say something about social security in my country (old-age pensions, medical care, etc.). ☐ Yes ☐ No
15. I can tell him what sort of government we have in my country. ☐ Yes ☐ No

29. I can describe weather-conditions in the four seasons in my own country. ☐ Yes ☐ No
30. I can tell him where he can eat and drink. ☐ Yes ☐ No

Total number of crosses: — Yes — No

Evaluation: If your total number of Yes crosses is [25] or above, and if your judgement of your own language ability is fairly accurate, you are likely to have reached Threshold Level in English.

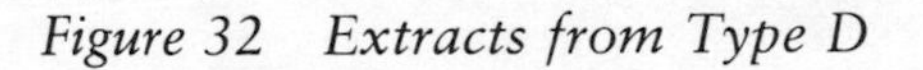

Figure 32 Extracts from Type D

Self-assessment form (Type E)

[To be translated into the learner's native language]

Instructions: Below you will find a number of statements concerning things that one can express in the language. Each statement is followed by two examples. Indicate your estimated command of the language by putting a cross in the appropriate box (YES or NO). Note that the sentences after the statements are *examples* only. If you can say the same thing in a similar way, you should put the cross in the YES box.

1. I can ask a person if he or she is of the same opinion as I am. ☐ Yes ☐ No
   Do you agree?
   Don't you think so?

8. I can express disappointment. ☐ Yes ☐ No
   That's a great pity.
   I am very sorry to hear that.

14. I can ask others to do something. ☐ Yes ☐ No
    Would you please give me a hand?
    Can I have this shirt washed, please?

20. I can express approval. ☐ Yes ☐ No
    Good!
    That's fine!

Total number of crosses: — Yes — No

Evaluation: If your total number of Yes crosses is above fifteen, and if your judgement of your own language ability is fairly accurate, you are likely to have reached Threshold Level in English.

Figure 33 Extracts from Type E

Type E (see figure 33) tests the learner's command of language functions from the Threshold Level.

The following example is from the Lothian Regional Project on Graded Levels of Achievement in Foreign Language Learning (GLAFLL) (see example 6 in Chapter 8). Clark (1980) states that the GLAFLL assessment programme is designed to increase motivation, and therefore assessment and methodology are regarded as inseparable. There are five assessment ingredients in the scheme:

- An explicit syllabus which was constructed partly on the basis of replies to 4,000 questionnaires from pupils in Lothian schools. The syllabus makes the learning objectives clear.
- A sub-syllabus with the pupil involved in negotiating what to learn and when to learn it.
- Record cards (of achievement) which list short-term goals. The pupil decides when he wants to be tested on these goals.
- Waystage Tests (school-based achievement tests – see figure 34). Once again the pupil decides when he is ready for it.
- Stage Tests I to IV, which are 'holistic' proficiency tests, conducted on a regional basis.

WAYSTAGE 1

Tick off in the Pupil column each of the following Language Activities when you are sure that you can do it.

Ask your teacher to tick the Teacher column once you have proved that you can do it.

	Pupil	Teacher
Address people, greet them, enquire after their health, say how you feel		
Say goodbye		
Thank someone		
Answer 'Yes', 'No', 'Perhaps', 'I don't know'		
Ask someone's name, give one's name		
Say 'I don't understand' and ask for repetition		
Ask for information and give information about family		
Ask the way to well-known places		
Count from 1 to 10		
Ask for simple food and drink in a shop		
Understand how the money system operates		

Figure 34

Social English

Another example of a check-list, partly based on Clark (1980) is that developed by Jackson (1981). This was developed as a check-list of aspects of social English for learners who had recently arrived in Britain and were adjusting to a very different way of life conducted through a foreign language. The students were asked to complete three questionnaires over one year (see figure 35). The first was to be completed during the first three months of residence, the second during the next four months, and the third in the next four months.

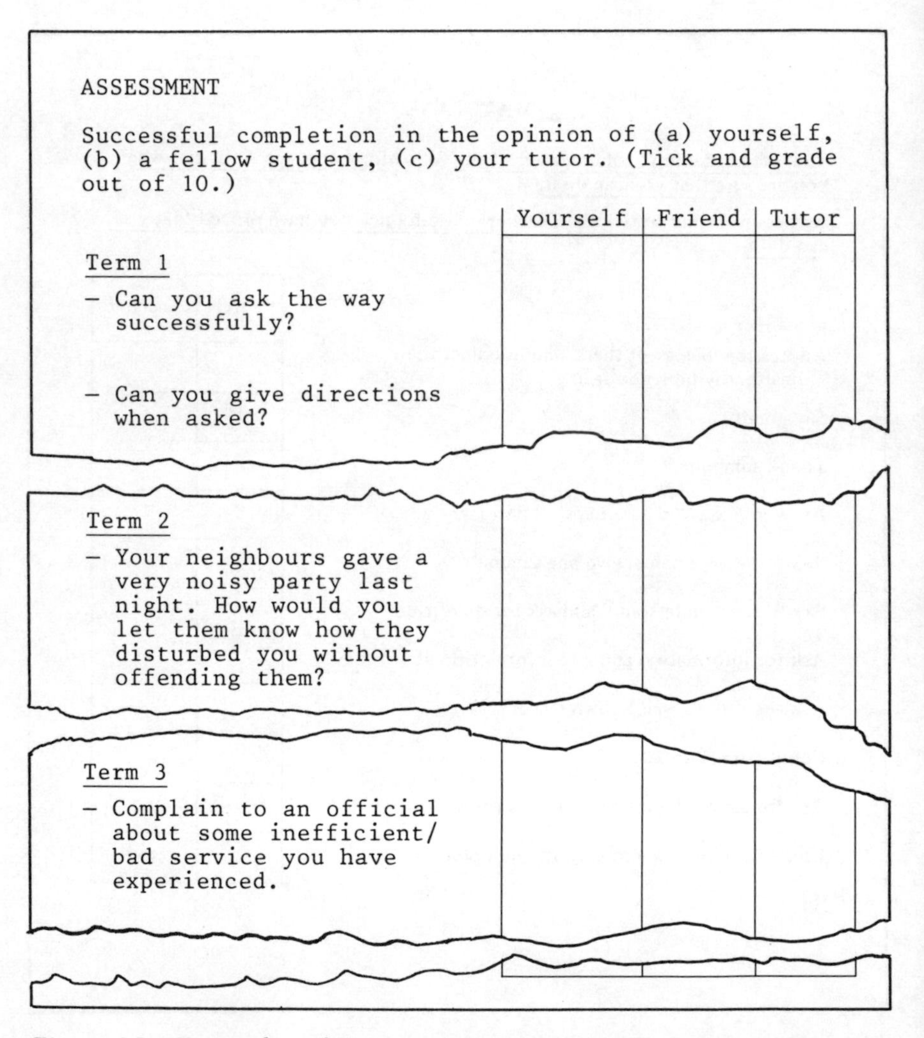

ASSESSMENT

Successful completion in the opinion of (a) yourself, (b) a fellow student, (c) your tutor. (Tick and grade out of 10.)

	Yourself	Friend	Tutor
Term 1			
– Can you ask the way successfully?			
– Can you give directions when asked?			
Term 2			
– Your neighbours gave a very noisy party last night. How would you let them know how they disturbed you without offending them?			
Term 3			
– Complain to an official about some inefficient/ bad service you have experienced.			

Figure 35 Examples of questions from the Jackson questionnaires

Self-assessment of structural and stylistic accuracy

Carver's (1982b) questionnaire is designed to assist users to make an estimate of their structural and stylistic accuracy. It is designed for Arabic speakers, and concentrates on areas of the language they have trouble with (see figure 36).

GRAMMAR

'Wh-' questions

1. Can you correct these sentences?
   - *Where Huda lives?
   - *Why you bought so much rice?
   - *When you will return?
   - *How many times you have been to Saudi Arabia?
2. Can you ask 'wh-' questions, (questions beginning when, where, why, how, etc. about topics such as:
   - the town which your friends come from in Saudi Arabia
   - the places in which they live in Edinburgh
   - the countries your tutors have visited

Write down some of these questions and show them to your tutors.

STYLE

Using 'and'

Can you improve the following paragraph:

Abdulaziz Ibn Saud founded the modern state of Saudi Arabia. And he was one of the great statesmen of the twentieth century. And he united the people of the Arabian peninsula. And in 1932 he became the first ruler of the country. And his son Fahd is today the fifth king of Saudi Arabia.

- Can you explain how you have improved the paragraph?
- Are you careful not to use 'and' too much when you write English?
- Do your tutors agree? Ask them.

Figure 36 Extracts from Carver's questionnaire

Informal self-assessment devices

Informal devices refer to those things some learners develop to help them to test their degree of success in some communicative event, or their present level of proficiency in one or other of the language skills. They include things like estimating the success of an oral communication in terms of the responses of an interlocutor's facial expression and so on (see example 12 in Chapter 8); making a rough estimate at the level of reading proficiency by attempting to read a newspaper; estimating one's level in writing ability by writing business letters and getting someone to comment on them (see example 9 in Chapter 8); and estimating one's level of listening comprehension by viewing video recordings and listening to the radio and audio recordings (see example 13 in Chapter 8).

We can suppose that all learners develop devices of this sort to a greater or lesser degree, but learners can be helped to refine such devices into more efficient ways of making estimates of their competence through training. Moulden (1982:28) suggests a number of ways that learners can be helped to improve their informal self-assessment devices through being made more aware of the component skills and abilities involved. Thus, in setting out to test *reading ability* the learner has first to decide which aspects he wants to test; the possibilities include reading speed, global comprehension, detailed and selective comprehension. These need to be considered together with the nature of the text, that is, whether it is literary, technical, commercial and so on. In self-testing *listening*, the learner first needs to become aware of the specific problems and advantages of different channels (for example, face-to-face, phone, radio, and television). The learner then needs to test specified listening skills (for example, listening efficiency – how often do you need to repeat, rephrasing etc.), global comprehension, detailed comprehension and selective comprehension. Testing one's *speaking skill* involves testing for grammatical, social and phonological correctness, communicative appropriateness, fluency and the speaker's compensation tactics. Testing for *writing* involves grammatical and lexical correctness and communicative appropriateness.

Moulden notes 'that the level to be attained for a given criterion is the learner's business. Definition of the level should be attempted, however crudely (for example, n% comprehension; absence of glassy-eyed look on the face of the person listening) so that there is a goal to aim at.'

Learner record keeping procedures

Record keeping procedures are not strictly self-assessment devices, but record keeping either implies that some form of assessment or monitoring has gone on in the recent past, or the process of making a record – of, for example, the units of a course which have been completed – can include a self-rating scheme.

Learner diaries

Carver and Dickinson (1981) suggest that the record of work should have the following headings:

- Date
- Lesson in text book
- Main activities
- How I performed
- What difficulties I had
- What difficulties I still have
- What I intend to do next

The form of the record keeping is important and thought needs to be given to the design of the system and how it is introduced to learners. The most important consideration is simplicity. The user must be able to understand the categories and be able to complete the record keeping quickly and easily.

The use of the term 'Diary' suggests a private document for the use of the learner only. This is appropriate for fully autonomous learners, but for those who are not fully autonomous, such as those who are studying in an institution with the help of a tutor, or who are working in a conventional class with some self-instructional elements, the learner diary will be more effective if it is available to the tutor. Carver and Dickinson suggest that the diary can be used in several ways, for example, during individual counselling, for guiding the learner in selecting material, and for guiding the learner in self-assessment.

Continuous self-assessment

Oskarsson (1984) also suggests record keeping by the learner and proposes a detailed form for this purpose (see figure 37).

→

1. In the last few lessons (days, weeks) we/I have studied/practised/worked on...

a) ....
b) ....
c) ....
d) ....
e) ....
f) ....

Fill in the empty spaces with topics and areas of study that are relevant in your case, for example:
a) pronunciation of words containing the sound /θ/
b) how to greet people
c) questions with do/does

2. How well do you master the above topics according to your own estimate?

	not at all	to some extent	fairly well	very well	completely
a)	□	□	□	□	□
b)	□	□	□	□	□
c)	□	□	□	□	□
d)	□	□	□	□	□
e)	□	□	□	□	□
f)	□	□	□	□	□

9. I judge my weak points to be the following:

....

....

Follow-up

Discuss your assessment and your points of view with a fellow student or in a small group, or with your teacher. Try to find out whether others think you tend to overestimate or underestimate your ability and acquired skills and then decide whether you ought to reconsider and readjust your 'yardstick'. Compare your subjective impressions with other criteria such as test scores, your teacher's evaluation, estimates by your fellow students.

Figure 37 Extracts from Oskarsson's form

Appendix D(II) Self- and peer-assessment of composition

Groups of learners (a group may be two or more) write compositions on appropriate themes and assess them as follows:

- The writer makes photocopies of the composition ideally for each member of the group.
- Each group member, including the writer, assesses the composition against a set of criteria supplied by the tutor (an example of a set of criteria is included after this description). This is done individually.
- The group then meets with the following two purposes, firstly to compare grades/marks awarded and to justify them according to the criteria. Secondly, and more importantly, each member of the group must make at least one suggestion for the improvement of the composition.
- Optionally the writer can then rewrite the composition incorporating the suggestions.

The tutor can take part in the assessment procedure on the same basis as other members of the group, that is, he can give a grade and be ready to justify it. If it is possible for the discussion of the grading and the suggestions for improvement to be carried out in the target language, this constitutes very valuable, and totally authentic, communication practice.

Sample evaluation criteria for compositions

This scheme assumes that composition writers will go through three stages: planning, rough draft and final draft, and so the total scheme is probably most suited to post-intermediate and advanced students. The criteria for the planning and rough draft stages are for the writer alone, though they could be used between the writer and tutor as guides in any consultation on the composition. The scheme for assessing the final draft would be used for the group assessment exercise suggested above. The criteria that follow could be translated into the learners' mother tongue if this was feasible and necessary. Alternatively the English may have to be simplified and each criterion explained to the group.

Planning the composition: self-evaluation questions

- Have I determined who my audience is?
- Have I taken an identifiable attitude towards my subject?

– Have I planned the composition to suit this audience?
– Have I listed ideas for my composition?
– Have I arranged the ideas into paragraphs?
– Have I decided on the order of paragraphs?
– Does my introductory paragraph tell my readers what is in the composition?
– Have I decided on a conclusion?

Rough draft

– Is the purpose/topic of the composition set out clearly in the introduction?
– Is the purpose/topic of the composition clear to my audience?
– Does each paragraph contribute to this purpose?
– Is each of my ideas illustrated with several details and/or examples?
– Is there a logical development from paragraph to paragraph?
– Is there a beginning, middle and end?
– Have I checked thoroughly for spelling errors?
– Have I checked for grammatical and other errors?*

Composition criteria for final draft

Organisation

1 The composition has an introduction which
  – informs the reader what the composition is about;
  – functions as a set of signposts to the reader, and/or
  – shows how the topic will be developed, and
  – may arouse interest.
2 The composition has a conclusion which
  – summarises the content of the composition, and/or
  – reaches an appropriate judgement on the basis of the arguments in the body of the composition.

The body of the composition

CONTENT
– The content is relevant to the subject of the composition.
– There is an adequate quantity of relevant points.

* These criteria and certain other aspects of the scheme were adapted from Lynch (1982).

ORGANISATION

- The composition has a clear system of organisation appropriate to the topic.
- The writer develops the argument in the composition.
- The writer guides the reader through the arguments.
- The writer supports arguments and generalisations with evidence.
- The writer keeps to the point.
- Each paragraph has a topic sentence and an expansion.
- There is a clear distinction between the main point and the examples.

POINT OF VIEW

- It is evident who the writer's audience is.
- The point of view adopted is appropriate to the audience.
- The point of view is clear.
- The point of view is maintained consistently, or there are clear reasons why it changes.

STYLE

- The writer has selected the correct level of formality for the topic and the audience.
- There are no/few lapses from the appropriate level of formality.
- The vocabulary is well selected for the formality level and the subject.

FORMAL STRUCTURE

- There are no/few errors of syntax.
- Errors have a moderate effect on understanding.
- Errors have a significant effect on understanding.
- All sentences are complete (no fragments, clauses without verbs etc.).
- Vocabulary is varied and appropriate.
- Cohesion markers are correctly used.
- Sentences are varied in structure and length.
- There is an appropriate use of idioms.

SPELLING AND PUNCTUATION

- Free of errors.
- Few errors.
- Many errors.

Bibliography

Ager, D.E., Clavering, E., and Galleymore, J. 1980. 'Assisted self-tutoring in foreign languages at Aston'. *Recherches et Echanges*, 5: 16–29.

Allwright, R.L. 1979. 'Abdication and responsibility in language teaching', *Studies in Second Language Acquisition*, 2: 105–21.

Allwright, R.L. 1982. 'Perceiving and pursuing learners' needs' in Geddes and Sturtridge, pp. 24–31.

Altman, H.B., and James, C.V. (eds.) 1980. *Foreign Language Teaching: Meeting Individual Needs.* Papers from the First Pergamon Institute of English Seminar, Oxford 1979. Pergamon Press.

Altman, H.B., and Politzer, R.L. 1971. *Individualizing Foreign Language Instruction. Final Report.* US Department of Health Education and Welfare, ERIC Documents ED 051 722.

Bachman, J.G. 1964. 'Motivation in a task situation as a function of ability and control over the task', *Journal of Abnormal and Social Psychology*, 69: 272–81.

Bartley, D.E. 1979. *The Adult Basic Education TESOL Handbook*. Collier Macmillan.

Beswick, N.W. 1972. Schools Council Working Paper 43. Evans/Methuen Educational.

Beswick, N.W. 1975. *Organising Resources: Six Case Studies.* The Final Report of the Schools Council Resource Centre Project. Heinemann Educational Books.

Blake, T. 1982. 'Storage and retrieval systems for self-access centres' in Geddes and Sturtridge.

Blundell, L., and Stokes, J. 1981. *Task Listening*. Cambridge University Press.

Bockman, J.F. 1971. 'The process of contracting' in Altman and Politzer, pp. 119–22.

Bockman, J.F., and Bockman V.M. 1972. 'The management of individualized programmes' in Gougher.

Boud, D. (ed.) 1981. *Developing Student Autonomy in Learning*. Kogan Page.

The British Council 1978. *Individualisation in Language Learning*, ELT Documents, 103.

The British Council (Pickett, G.D.) 1978. *The Foreign Language Learning Process*, ETIC Occasional Paper.

Brown, H.D. 1973. 'Affective variables in second language acquisition', *Language Learning*, 23: 231–44.

Brown, S. 1980. 'Self-access at Saffron Walden', Appendix 1 in Sturtridge and Bolitho.

Carroll, E.R., McLennan, R., Boyd-Bowman, P., and Gougher, R.L. 1971. 'Report and recommendations of the committee on adapting existing materials to individualized instruction' in Altman and Politzer.

Carver, D.J. 1982a. Introduction to 'The selection and training of helpers' in Cousin (ed.) (1982a).

Carver, D.J. 1982b. 'Self-assessment questionnaire for Saudi Arabian students', Moray House (mimeo).

Carver, D.J. 1984. 'Plans, learner strategies and self-direction in language learning', *System*, 12: 123–31.

Carver, D.J., and Dickinson, L. 1981. 'Autonomie, apprentissage, autodirige et domain affectif dans l'apprentissage des langues en milieu scolaire', *Etudes de Linguistique Appliquée*, 4: 39–63.

Carver, D.J., and Dickinson, L. 1982a. 'Learning to be self-directed' in Geddes and Sturtridge.

Carver, D.J., and Dickinson L. 1982b. *Self-directed Learning. Collected Papers in Self-directed Learning in English Language Learning.* Moray House (mimeo).

Chaix, P., and O'Neil, C. 1978. *A Critical Analysis of Forms of Autonomous Learning (Autodidaxy and Semi-autonomy) in the Field of Foreign Language Learning. Final Report.* UNESCO Doc Ed 78/WS/58.

Chastain, K. 1975. 'An examination of the basic assumptions of "individualized" instruction', *Modern Language Journal*, 59: 334–44.

Clark, J. 1980. 'Lothian Region's project on graded levels of achievement in foreign language learning: from principles to practice', *Modern Languages in Scotland*, 19: 61–74.

Cohen, A.D. 1983. 'Reformulating compositions', *TESOL Newsletter*, 17: 1–5.

Cohen, A.D. 1985. 'What can we learn from the language learner?' Paper given to TESOL Scotland 1985.

Cohen, A.D., and Aphek, E. 1981. 'Easifying second language learning', *Studies in Second Language Acquisition*, 3: 221–36.

Cousin, W.D. (ed.) 1982a. 'Report of the workshops in the role and training of helpers for self-access language learning systems'. Moray House (mimeo).

Cousin, W.D. 1982b. 'Experience of being a helper on the British Council Summer School for foreign teachers of English held at Stirling University', Appendix 1, Aims and objectives questionnaire in Cousin (ed.) (1982a).

Cousin, W.D. 1985. 'From freedom to learn to evaluation and accountability. Whither the 1980s?' Theme paper: definition and setting up of a resource centre, TESOL Conference 1985.

Cousin, W.D., Dauer, R., Dickinson, N., and Moor, C.J. 1980. 'Self-directed learning in English as a foreign language: aims and objectives', Annex 1 of Holec.

Cross, D. 1980. 'Personalised language learning' in Altman and James.

Dalwood, M. 1977. 'The reciprocal language course', *Audio Visual Language Journal*, 15: 73–80.

Dam, L. 1982. 'Beginning English – an experiment in learning and teaching'. Danmarks Laererhøjskole (mimeo).

Dam, L. 1983a. 'Intermediate English – an experiment in learning and teaching: evaluation'. Karlslunde Skole, Denmark (mimeo).

Dam, L. 1983b. 'Intermediate English – an experiment in learning and teaching. Expressed objectives – plans – activities'. Karleslunde Skole, Denmark (mimeo). (These monographs can be obtained from Leni Dam, Paedagogisk Central, Hundige Boulevard 11, 2670 Greve Strand, Denmark.)

de Leeuw, M., and E. 1965. *Read Better, Read Faster*. Penguin.

Dickinson, L. 1974. 'A student-centred approach to language laboratory methodology', *Pariser Werkstattgespräche Laborübungen Für Fortgeschrittene*. British Council and Goethe Institute, Paris.

Dickinson, L. 1976. 'Autonomy, self-directed learning and individualisation' in The British Council (1978) pp. 7–28.

Dickinson L. (ed.) 1980. 'Report of the workshops in self-directed language learning'. Moray House (mimeo).

Dickinson, L., and Carver, D.J. 1980. 'Learning how to learn: steps towards self-direction in foreign language learning in schools', ELT Journal, 35: 1–7.

Entwistle, N. 1977. 'Strategies of learning and studying: recent research findings', *British Journal of Educational Studies*, 25: 225–38.

Entwistle, N. 1981. *Styles of Learning and Teaching: An Integrated Outline of Educational Psychology for Students, Teachers and Lecturers*. John Wiley.

Flavell, J.H. 1979. 'Metacognition and cognitive monitoring. A new area of cognitive-developmental enquiry', *American Psychologist*, 34: 906–11.

Galleymore, J. 1976. 'Self-tutoring and assisted self-tutoring in modern languages at the University of Aston' in Harding-Esch (1976a).

Ganserhoff, K.A. 1979. 'The why, who and how of individualized instruction for adults' in Bartley (1979) pp. 62–9.

Gardner, R.C., and Lambert, W.E. 1972. *Attitudes and Motivation in Second Language Learning*. Newbury House.

Gardner, R.C., and Smythe, P.C. 1975. 'Motivation and second language acquisition', *Canadian Modern Language Review*, 31: 218–30.

Geddes, M., and McAlpin, J. 1978. 'Activity options in language courses' in The British Council (1978) pp. 29–36.

Geddes, M., and Sturtridge, G. (eds.) 1982. *Individualisation*. Modern English Publications.

Gibbs, G. 1981. *Teaching Students to Learn: A Student-Centred Approach*. Open University Press.

Gougher, R. L. (ed.) 1972. *Individualization of Instruction in Foreign Languages. A Practical Guide*. Centre for Curriculum Development.

Gross, R. 1979. *The Lifelong Learner*. Simon and Schuster.

Harding, E., and Tealby, A. 1981. 'Counselling for language learning at the University of Cambridge: progress report on an experiment', *Mélanges Pédagogiques*: pp. 95–120.

Harding-Esch, E. (ed.) 1976a. *Self-directed Learning and Autonomy*. Report of a seminar held at the University of Cambridge, 13–15 December 1976. University of Cambridge, Department of Linguistics and CRAPEL (mimeo).

Harding-Esch, E. 1976b. 'Of some limits to autonomous programmes in language learning' in Harding-Esch (1976a).

Harding-Esch, E. 1982. 'The Open Access Sound and Video Library of the University of Cambridge: progress report and development', *System*, 10: 13–28.

Heidt, E.U. 1979. *Self-evaluation in Learning: A Report on Trends, Experiences and Research Findings.* UNESCO Division of Structures, Content, Method and Techniques of Education.
Hendrickson, J.M. 1980. 'Listening and speaking activities for foreign language learners', *Canadian Modern Language Review*, 36: 735–48.
Hendrickson, J.M. 1983. 'Listening and speaking activities for foreign language learners: second collection', *Canadian Modern Language Review*, 39: 267–84.
Heron, J. 1981. 'Assessment revisited' in Boud.
Hilsum, S., and Strong, G. 1978. *The Secondary Teacher's Day.* NFER-NELSON.
Holec, H. 1980. *Autonomy and Foreign Language Learning.* Council of Europe.
Hosenfeld, C. 1975. 'The new student role: individual differences and implications for instruction' in American Council on Teaching Foreign Languages (ACTFL), *Review of Foreign Language Instruction.* National Textbook Co.
Hudson, L. (ed.) 1970. *The Ecology of Human Intelligence.* Penguin.
Jackson, M.G. 1981. 'Self-assessment in oral skills for Saudi Arabian students', Moray House (mimeo).
Knowles, M.S. 1975. *Self-directed Learning. A Guide for Learners and Teachers.* Association Press.
Little, D., and Davis E. 1986. 'Interactive video for language learning: The Autotutor Project', *System*, 14: 29–34.
Logan, G.E. 1980. 'Individualized foreign language instruction: American patterns for accommodating learner differences in the classroom' in Altman and James.
Lynch, D. 1982. 'Easing the process: a strategy for evaluating compositions', *College Composition and Communication*, 33: 310–14.
Mackenzie, N., Postgate, R., and Scupham, J. 1975. *Open Learning Systems and Problems in Post-secondary Education.* The UNESCO Press.
McCafferty, J.B.(ND) *A Consideration of a Self-access Approach to the Learning of English.* The British Council (mimeo).
McCafferty, J.B. 1982. 'Self-access: problems and proposals' in Carver and Dickinson (1982b: 43–7).
McDonough, S.H. 1978. 'The foreign language learning process: introspection and generalisation' in The British Council (1978).
McDonough, S.H. 1981. *Psychology in Foreign Language Teaching.* George Allen and Unwin.
Morsman, I. 1980. 'Guide to the study centre' in Sturtridge and Bolitho.
Moulden, H. 1982. 'The need for helpers and their roles at different language learning levels' in Cousin (1982a) pp. 20–7.
Moulden, H. 1985. 'Extending self-directed learning of English in an engineering college' in Riley (ed.) (1985).
Munby, J. 1978. *Communicative Syllabus Design.* Cambridge University Press.
Naiman, N., Fröhlich, M., Stern, H.H., and Todesco, A. 1978. *The Good Language Learner.* Research in Education Series, 7. Ontario Institute for Studies in Education.
Nisbet, J., and Shucksmith, J. 1984. 'The seventh sense. Reflections on learning to learn'. Scottish Council for Research in Education.

Oskarsson M. 1980. *Approaches to Self-assessment in Foreign Language Learning*. Pergamon Press.
Oskarsson, M. 1984. 'Self-assessment of foreign language skills. A survey of research and development work'. University of Göteborg (mimeo).
Partlett, M.L. 1970. 'The syllabus-bound student' in Hudson.
Pickett, G.D. 1978. (See The British Council.)
Pirsig, R.M. 1974. *Zen and the Art of Motorcycle Maintenance*. Corgi.
Riley, P. 1974. 'From fact to function: aspects of the work of the CRAPEL'. *Mélanges Pédagogiques*: pp. 1–12.
Riley, P. 1980. 'Learner exercise and self-assessment techniques'. CRAPEL (mimeo).
Riley, P. 1981. 'Pedagogical implications of the use of authentic documents'. CRAPEL (mimeo).
Riley, P. (ed.) 1985. *Discourse and Learning*. Longman.
Riley, P., and Zoppis, C. 1976. 'The Sound and Video Library. An interim report on an experiment'. *Mélanges Pédagogiques*: pp. 125–43.
Roberts, R. 1975. 'The *session libre*', *Audio Visual Language Journal*, 13: 3–11.
Rodgers, T.S. 1979. 'Towards a model of learner variation in autonomous foreign language learning'. *Papers in Second Language Acquisition*, 2: 73–97.
Rogers, C.R. 1969. *Freedom to Learn*. Merrill Press.
Rubin, J. 1981. 'Study of cognitive processes in second language learning', *Applied Linguistics*, 2: 117–31.
Schumann, J.H. 1975. 'Affective factors and the problem of age in second language acquisition', *Language learning*, 25: 209–35.
Scott, M., Carioni, L., Zanatta, M., Bayer, E., and Quintanilha, T. 1984. 'Using a "standard exercise" in teaching reading comprehension', *ELT Journal*, 38: 114–20.
Smith, R.M. 1983. *Learning How to Learn: Applied Theory for Adults*. Open University Press.
Stanchina, C. 1975. 'The logic of autonomy as a strategy for adult learners'. CRAPEL (mimeo).
Stanchina, C. 1976. 'Autonomy at work with adults', in Harding-Esch (1976a).
Stanchina, C., and Riley, P. 1978. 'Aspects of autonomous learning', The British Council (1978): pp. 76–97.
Stern, H.H. 1983. *Fundamental Concepts of Language Teaching*. Oxford University Press.
Stevick, E.W. 1982. *Teaching Languages: A Way and Ways*. Newbury House.
Sturtridge, G. 1982. 'Individualised learning: what are the options for the classroom teacher?' in Geddes and Sturtridge.
Sturtridge, G., and Bolitho, R. 1980. *Individualised and Self-access Materials*. Report of a Workshop. Bell College, Saffron Walden (mimeo).
Tough, A. 1971, 1979. *The Adults' Learning Projects: A Fresh Approach to Theory and Practice in Adult Learning*. (2nd Edn.) The Ontario Institute for Studies in Education.
Trim, J.L.M. 1980. Foreword of Oskarsson (1980).
van Ek, J.A. 1976. *The Threshold Level for Modern Language Teaching in Schools*. Longman.

von Elek, T. 1982. 'Test of Swedish as a second language: an experiment in self-assessment'. Work papers from the Language Teaching Research Centre, 31. University of Gothenburg.

Wesche, M.B. 1979. 'Learning behaviours of successful adult students on intensive language training', *Canadian Modern Language Review*, 35: 415–30.

Wilson, J. 1981. *Student Learning in Higher Education*. Croom Helm.

Windeatt, S. 1981. 'A project for self-access learning for English language and study skills', *Practical Papers in English Language Education*, 3. University of Lancaster.

Acknowledgements

The author and publishers are grateful to the following for permission to reproduce copyright material:

p. 14, fig. 2, L. Dickinson, from ELT Document 103, *Individualisation in Language Learning*, copyright The British Council 1976; **pp. 52–3,** fig. 6, **p. 54,** fig. 7 and **p. 89,** fig. 20, J.B. McCafferty; **p. 62,** fig. 11, **p. 63,** fig. 13 and **p. 64,** fig. 14, L. Dam; **pp. 73–7,** Cambridge University Press for extracts from L. Blundell and J. Stokes, *Task Listening*, 1981, Student's Book p. 38 and Teacher's Book pp. 96 and 93–4; **pp. 92, 94,** Modern English Publications for R.L. Allwright, 'Needs questionnaire' and 'Language learning strategies' from M. Geddes and G. Sturtridge (eds.) *Individualisation*, 1978, pp. 25 and 27; **pp. 96–7,** figs. 23 and 24 and **p. 117,** fig. 27 reprinted with permission from *System* vol. 10, Harding-Esch, 'Needs analysis' copyright 1982 Pergamon Journals Ltd.; **p. 113,** fig. 26, P. Riley; **p. 128,** fig. 28, J. Nisbet and J. Shucksmith; **pp. 170–1,** Oxford University Press for M. Scott *et al.*, 'The Standard Reading Exercise', *English Language Teaching Journal* vol. 38, 1984; **p. 178,** fig. 31, T. von Elek; **pp. 179–80,** figs. 32–3, M. Oskarsson; **p. 181,** fig. 34, J. Clark; **p. 182,** fig. 35, M. G. Jackson; **p. 183,** fig. 36, D.J. Carver.

Index